Enigma in Many Keys

Enigma in Many Keys

◆

The Life and Letters of a WWII Intelligence Officer

Robert E. Button

iUniverse, Inc.
New York Lincoln Shanghai

Enigma in Many Keys
The Life and Letters of a WWII Intelligence Officer

All Rights Reserved © 2004 by Robert E. Button

No part of this book may be reproduced or transmitted in any form or by any means, graphic, electronic, or mechanical, including photocopying, recording, taping, or by any information storage retrieval system, without the written permission of the publisher.

iUniverse, Inc.

For information address:
iUniverse, Inc.
2021 Pine Lake Road, Suite 100
Lincoln, NE 68512
www.iuniverse.com

ISBN: 0-595-32157-7 (pbk)
ISBN: 0-595-66481-4 (cloth)

Printed in the United States of America

*For my British warbride, Decima,
and our daughters, Phyllis and Marilyn.*

Many years later, when everything was business, when he worked harder than anyone in a country whose values are structured on hard work, he believed that life, true life, was something that was stored in music. True life was kept safe in the lines of Tchaikovsky's *Eugene Onegin* while you went out into the world and met the obligations required of you.

—Ann Patchett, *Bel Canto*

Contents

Foreword xi
1 Early Years 1
2 Entering Business 7
3 Before the War 17
4 Northern Ireland 31
5 London and Bletchley Park 47
6 Letters from London 61
7 France 91
8 Letters from France 97
9 Luxembourg 117
10 Letters from Luxembourg 125
11 Germany 135
12 Letters from Germany 139
13 Life after Enigma 167
14 Diplomacy in Paris 179
15 New Era of Communications 185
16 Connecticut Music 197
Epilogue 205

Foreword

WITH CHARACTERISTIC MODESTY and charm, retired U.S. Army Colonel Robert Button weaves a wry wit and a degree of mystery into his life story, *Enigma in Many Keys*. A talented piano player, Bob arranges the narrative of his career as he does his music: allowing the various strains of his life to mingle into harmony. From the "Ultra" top-secret ranks of World War II intelligence and high levels of diplomatic and civil service to the executive back rooms of broadcasting and a front seat at the launch of the first communications satellite, Bob Button has found himself in the right place at the right time with the right talents.

Throughout the European campaign he was responsible for the safe handling of highly secret Ultra intelligence obtained in Bletchley Park, England, where German codes and ciphers, including Enigma, were successfully broken. A large part of Bob's autobiography is of his war years as recalled from memory and recorded in letters written to his parents from 1941-1945. Erudite letters track his life from U.S. Army draftee to senior intelligence liaison officer, from the UK through France on D-day +2 to the liberation of Paris, and eventually through Germany after the surrender. These remarkable letters, by a soldier in his 20's, are perceptive and detailed, and give a look at what went on outside of battle. In them we get a discerning yet sympathetic perspective of the Northern Irish, the English, and the continental Europeans. Bob shows a close affinity for the English, strengthened by the times he was attached to the 2nd British Army while serving under General Bradley and others in the U.S. high command, and culminating in his marriage to British songstress Decima Knight. The harmony created by this musical duo still entertains many loyal fans in their hometown of Old Greenwich, Connecticut.

Enigma in Many Keys complements other recollections of World War II, with its focus away from the brutal tragedies of battle. Rich descriptions and keen insights result from the author's access to important people and places. Bob tells us, for example, about the Irish castle owners, London society folks, members of the British War Cabinet, and top American military commanders in whose company he moved. These characters became the subjects of his letters home, and their memorable interactions and idiosyncrasies intertwined with musical and literary allusions make this a unique account of the war.

A dynamic interplay of chance and intelligent effort has characterized Bob's life and career. Add a warm tune on the piano keys as background and you have an autobiography original in its approach and content, and a welcome addition to the World War II canon.

In a letter to a friend, Dr. Samuel Johnson wrote, "Language is the clothes of thought." Bob Button brings his wartime thoughts and experiences to life in *Enigma in Many Keys* using phrases of elegant simplicity from that vast and varied wardrobe that is the English language. It is good to see it in print.

Peter Wescombe
Trustee, Bletchley Park Trust
Buckinghamshire, England

Acknowledgements

For whatever I have accomplished in the journey herein related, I acknowledge the help and inspiration of a stable and affectionate family and the encouragement of some extraordinary friends. My immediate family, consisting of my wife Decima, daughters Phyllis and Marilyn; along with my sister, Anne Hart, constantly urged me to record my experiences up to and through the Enigma looking-glass and beyond. This book owes its inception to them.

I am indebted to Sir Arthur C. Clarke, whose writings enabled me to intellectually escape the confines of this earth, and to Hubert J. Schlafly, who led me through the technical means of doing so. The musical accompaniment to my life has been and continues to be provided by companions in my band, singing and soloist troupes—to all of whom I give my thanks and great appreciation. And finally, my writer's muse, Joanne Dearcopp, deserves special mention. Equally at home in many fields, she knew how to inspire, to clarify the various aspects of my life, and to ingeniously blend diverse material into one whole story.

1

Early Years

AS FAR AS I know, no cosmic or environmental events attended my birth. It was in the month of July 1915, and World War I had just started. Austro-German troops had just invaded Poland, so it came as no surprise to me when, in 1939, they reverted to their old tricks to launch World War II—"my" war. Woodrow Wilson was president of the United States, and the country's economy offered gas at eight cents per gallon. The Boston Red Sox won the World Series over Philadelphia and the average price for a new automobile that year was about five hundred dollars.

I was the second of four children. Our home was in Maplewood, New Jersey, a commuter refuge for New York stockbrokers served by a steam railroad, which took people to Hoboken, where they crossed the Hudson on very dilapidated ferryboats, which I think are still running. It was an exciting trip for a youth, and it shaped my thoughts to the extent that I grew up believing that the most important spot in the world was not Bethlehem or Rome or Washington, but simply and clearly Wall Street.

My father started as a salesman for the Columbia Phonograph Company (later to become CBS) of which my great uncle, Edward Easton, was then chairman. Father was also a weekend warrior-in-training for America's entry into the war, which everyone assumed was inevitable. My mother was what mothers were expected to be in those days: a meticulous housewife, an excellent cook, and a consistent churchgoer. In addition, she was a talented pianist, a well-traveled protégé of a prominent family in New Jersey, and a student of cultural history. In spite of this lineage I did not inherit a driving ambition to become a salesman, a musician, or a soldier. In fact, the three career paths seemed irreconcilable. As it turned out in the end, I would become all three, with music having the greatest and most lasting influence, while salesmanship provided the elements of life support. As for the military, it was the last thing on my mind.

There is little to record of substance about my early years, with one exception. As I only learned at a much later date, at the age of two I contracted pneumonia and the doctor gave up on me as a lost cause. My parents sought the assistance of a Baptist prayer group, who attended at my bedside. One moment in the course of their service, I have been told, my infant body broke out in a profuse sweat and the pneumonia departed completely. My parents only reluctantly ever referred to this incident, but its authenticity is beyond doubt and its characteristics not unknown to the medical or clerical professions. It was my first encounter with a benevolent Providence that has stayed with me all my life.

Somehow I learned to read and write ahead of my ordinary level in school and so I bypassed the third grade. My reading was mostly in history; my earliest hero was Sir Frances Drake, and my earliest villains the Spanish Inquisitors, the menace of which I never ceased to worry about right down to the days of Senator Joseph McCarthy. At Maplewood High School, I was a track star, which in a sense belied a certain phlegmatic disposition. My family observed that, "He may run fast, but it takes a gun to start him." In high school, I was elected president of my senior class and achieved high enough grades to earn a place in a very selective college.

For some reason my mother was insistent that I should become a pianist. She was an accomplished pianist herself, and I knew she had had a beau, prominent in the world of classical music, named Edwin Hughes, of New York. Perhaps her idea was that I should emulate him and grow up in the salons of the devotees of opera and concerti. My father had other ideas; to him, the only real action in life took place on

Wall Street. He rode the prosperity boom to become a successful stockbroker with enough sagacity and good luck to survive the crash of 1929 without serious loss to most of his clients and relatives. His only concession to the musical aspirations of my mother was to take up the saxophone. He never made use of it in the popular music scene, but he would play hymns at the local church, with dubious effect on the worship service.

My father never related the stock market movements to our family situation, but one day he provided me with a lesson in basic economics that charted my course from then on. He offered me a dollar if I would learn a certain popular song on the piano. So I did, and he paid. Under protest from my music teacher and my mother, I began to pay more attention to Irving Berlin than to Bach, Beethoven, and Brahms because Berlin's music apparently was where the money was, Depression or no Depression. By the age of fourteen, I had a job with a small dance orchestra and found myself playing up to three or four in the morning, watching dancers cavort to the beat we were making. I was learning what it took to make partygoers feel lively and seductive at that hour of the night. There were no drugs then on which to get hooked. Instead, women were my drug of choice, my muses, my inspiration. (They still are.) After all, I reasoned, in ancient Greece the muses were women, and so they remained for me a legitimate source of inspiration, crucial to both my performance and my musical creations.

From my secure position at the piano, I was able to observe people at play. The women, in particular, seemed to express what the music suggested. Not so the men, who seemed to be mere accessories to the glamour of the ladies. Most of the requests made of our combo came from the women, and when we acceded, there seemed to be a certain complicity between the musicians and the ladies to enhance whatever plots the ladies had in mind at the moment. I began to grasp the connection between piano-playing and real life. I learned that people needed music and would pay for it, for pleasure, for inspiration, for dancing, marching, dining, and devotional services. Never again did anyone (not even Mother) have to coax me to sit down and diligently practice those scales and arpeggios that form the structure of musical proficiency.

All this practical experience in the performing arts suddenly became relevant when it appeared there was not enough money at home to provide a college education for four children. My older brother had graduated from medical school and achieved a doctor's practice, but when it was my turn, things looked doubtful. I was making my own money, however, and with the assistance of a scholarship plus a loan from the local Lions Club, I entered as a freshman at Dartmouth in the Class of 1936.

Now things began to get serious. I had to face scholastic, social, athletic, economic, and musical competition on a national scale, with some of the best that my generation of students could offer and at a time when the social structure of the nation was under severe strain, as were the family values within that structure. And I had to make a living as well, which I did mostly by playing piano with a nine-piece orchestra I formed with fellow classmates in my sophomore year. We called ourselves the Green Serenaders (green being the Dartmouth color) and were much in demand at college functions. We also played on the local radio station and at other colleges including Wellesley, Vassar, Skidmore, Colby, Williams, and Amherst.

Music was the engine driving this phase of my life. At vacation our orchestra would embark on a cruise liner from New York to the Caribbean or the Panama Canal. During summer vacations we traveled to Europe as ships' musicians, stag dance partners, and deckhands. Once there, we toured by bicycle and returned in time for the fall semester. Nowadays students take in the foreign scene as part of their study courses; we did it on our own, financed by tips from cruise passengers. We toured on foot and by bicycle, met the local population, discussed the deteriorating political scene, and added to our classroom education an understanding of the ominous realities of the world at that time. I learned more about life from these engagements than I did in any classroom.

Two significant developments grew out of these summer experiences abroad. One was that I came to know England, France, and Germany at close quarters, through their language, their music, and their people. The other was that I foresaw World War II in the making and started wondering what role I would play in it. On one of my vacations in Europe, I visited a German youth labor camp as the guest of an American company that had a German affiliate. There I saw young Germans vigorously at work strengthening their bodies, cleaning up their environment, and conducting military-like exercises under the swastika banner. I saw the German Army swear allegiance to Adolf Hitler and sensed the pride of the Nazis. I saw the newly built underground steel bunkers of eastern France that later became known as the Maginot Line—a grim expression of the smug, helpless, defensive mentality of the French, and, as it turned out, it was useless as well. After seeing what was happening on the continent, I reflected on the Oxford University students' anti–military service resolution, and I wondered if my British friends were actually asking for what they were soon to receive by their lack of preparedness.

I decided I would help England win if a war came. My attitude toward England may have been influenced by the fact that while on a summer vacation bicycling through Bavaria in 1934, I met an English girl, about my age, likewise doing a bicycle tour. Her interests, musical and other, seemed to coincide closely with mine. I concluded that if the Germans were to attack England, which it seemed they had in mind to do, my only possible course of action would be to rush to her defense. Indeed, this is about what happened some eight or nine years later.

Another vivid memory of that summer occurred during my bicycle tour of Germany. A few friends and I visited Oberammergau on the same weekend that Hitler and Goering had decided to appear as audience to the passion play of 1934. We sat in a side section of the amphitheater in the same row as the Nazi leaders. There were guards everywhere. Clearly, Adolf and Hermann thought of themselves, not Jesus, as the main attraction. They were out, trying to get votes, like any politician. Gun-toting security guards surrounded the two leaders but no one provoked an outbreak. After all, Hitler got his start in Bavaria. I often reflect on the fact that had I been a martyr, like some of our present-day terrorists, I could have blown up Hitler and Goering right then and there, but the thought never occurred to me at the time.

Watching a war gestate in 1936, among the same protagonists as were involved in 1914, led me to a certain cynicism about politics and history for which a college liberal arts education provided no answers. Neither did religion. The "here we go again" feeling provoked by the German sinking of the liner *Athena* left me in total doubt as to career direction or even survival. I had only a deep-seated intuition regarding the inevitability of a personal alliance with the British on some level. This instinct proved entirely accurate, although it was based less on politics than on a profound personal affinity for British culture, its history, and its people—especially one of them.

2

Entering Business

THERE SEEMED TO be no way to turn my college education into an appropriate and meaningful career in the face of the global convulsion I foresaw. I had no interest or talent in the technical professions. Nor had I the patience or the funding for three years of law school. And how could one enter the world of business as a piano player? I shut my eyes, held my breath, and grabbed the first offer that came my way. A friendly neighborhood banker had me placed as a junior credit investigator—an introduction to the profession of spying.

I do not mean to imply that my four years' experience at Dartmouth College was mainly a musical tour with educational overtones and romantic but irrelevant sidelights. I did achieve scholastic honors in English, athletic honors on the track team, and I was a star debater, president of my fraternity, and a member of Casque and Gauntlet, the senior honorary society. My bills were paid with money earned with the orchestra. I read widely and deeply; saw the world, learned German and French, and thought profoundly about Hitler, Mussolini, and the British. Never could I have guessed how all these elements of my formative years would come together in the impending world crisis. I could only watch, and try to relate to the business world in which I had been given an introductory role as a bank clerk.

The four years following my college graduation in 1936 were a descent from a high position on campus to the bottom of the economic ladder, from pride to despair, from a purposeful college life to an aimless, meaningless, and degrading wandering through a social and business wilderness. It seems I could not fit myself into the role expected of entry-level bank employees. In an effort to break out of that mold, I studied law at night for three long years but had even more trouble staying awake at law school than I did at the bank. When my employer found out that in my spare time I also played the piano in the evenings, it was obvious to him that I could not possibly be what he called "banking-minded." I was apparently a threat to the morale, the atmosphere, and the viability of the bank, possibly even to Wall Street itself. There could only be one outcome. I was fired. Years later, I wrote about this experience in *Greenwich Time*.

❖ ❖ ❖

My self-esteem was almost irreparably destroyed the day when, as an inevitable consequence of once having taken a job in a bank, I was then fired. Practically every attitude, every objective, even every personal habit, every aspect of appearance that had originally led me to a bank was wrongly conceived—and has now been altered or reversed, to my great good fortune. How I selected a bank for the honor of employing me is a complicated tale, but the story as to why the bank disengaged me is much more simple.

In the first place, I wore shoes that had only three eyelets for the laces, or sometimes even only two. This is not acceptable in banks. A former assistant secretary of the U.S. Treasury, himself a prominent banker, told me some years later that the first thing he looked at in sizing up a prospective employee was the number of eyelets in his shoes. Any fewer than five was a sure indication of a less than conservative nature, perhaps even an instability of character. How right he was!

With the few discretionary dollars I possessed, I never bought good sound stocks. I speculated in yen, pre-Revolutionary Russian bonds, or beryllium futures. The latter did me in. Nobody in those days knew anything about beryllium except one of my college economics professors, who informed me it was a strategic war material. When the bank learned that I had conceived the goal of cornering the beryllium market, just as the Harrimans once cornered copper (and just as my college professor had advised as the way to make a fortune), the bank considered this an aberration. Junior clerks did not do such things. Only the vice presidents or the directors could think such thoughts, and then only with sound, anti-trust legal advice. So this, with the shoe eyelets, put two strikes against me.

Banks provide opulent surroundings along with penurious salaries, at least in the beginning. Therefore junior clerks sometimes sought to augment their wages with outside activities, which might include delivering groceries, shoe-shining, washing windows, escort services, or, as in my case, piano-playing. For a while I managed this covertly. It would not be wise to be seen playing the piano in a West 44th Street bar where one of the bank vice presidents might be having an after-hours nip with a lady customer. I therefore resorted to disguise, a practical training, as it turned out, for a later semi-career with a certain intelligence service. But word soon got around that in addition to whatever I was doing in the bank, which I did not know myself, I was also a musician. Two more incompatible career paths cannot be imagined; a musician plays with and on emotions, whereas when a banker gently forecloses the widow's mortgage, emotion hardly figures in the transaction. The musician loves crowds, and he studies them. The banker hides from them. Behind every mob he sees the guillotine; his social outlook is symbolized by the gigantic steel door to his vault. I once suggested that a few drops of sulfuric acid in the lock would render the whole system inoperative. This was regarded as a very bad joke.

Thus there were at least three good reasons why I became known as a prime threat to the banking industry. The foregone conclusion was my separation, or firing, or sacking, as the British say. At the time, I felt that the bank was shortsighted. The industry, I thought, needed piano players, high rollers, some fellows with three-eyelet shoes, or shoes with no eyelets at all, with perhaps just a tassel, the ultimate in gaucherie. But my employers thought they needed young men with conservative low-profile attitudes, those who wore pinstriped underwear. I could change neither my image nor their attitudes. They won. Although, to my regret at the time, they lost a potential wizard banker, they later gained my account. I needed them more than they needed me.

They have everybody else's money, of course, and this is what banks are for. They remind one of the Black Hole in current literature on astronomy. In my frequent moments of fantasy I see, sitting at the bottom of this Black Hole, Alan Greenspan, chief of the Federal Reserve. All day long he juggles the last three ounces of pure gold in the universe. If he drops one, we have inflation, and your money becomes worth only half as much as it was before. If he drops the second, we have a recession and out come the soup kitchens to the corner of Broad and Wall. If he drops the third, we have had it. All our money and all the banks disappear into the Black Hole, except for one bank in the Cayman Islands, which has collected all the taxes of all the people with all the money that should have been paid to the authorities and which thus has become the central bank for the entire world, with Alec Guinness as its president.

My greatest regret, understandably, was that I did not think of becoming a banker in the Cayman Islands, or perhaps Liechtenstein, another place that gets rich on taxes owed and unpaid to everywhere else. But it was difficult to figure out how one made money anywhere else, outside of New York. All the money seemed to be there, and if it temporarily flowed out to Brazil or Peru, it sooner or later returned, as any Brazilian or Peruvian will tell you. I therefore stayed in New York, hoping that something else would turn up whereby I could get some of that money for myself. And so it did.

I presently found myself in the radio broadcasting business where two eyelet shoes, a willingness to gamble at great odds, and a reasonable instability of character were exactly the qualifications required. It was for me an easy adjustment, pleasant employment, and a welcome opportunity to dabble in the arts. Meanwhile my erstwhile bank employers, I discovered, were standing in queues outside the doors of the radio station waiting for a chance to buy the next available prime time thirty-second station break for their commercials. It was the ultimate balm to my humiliation at their hands when I found that one of my duties was to screen their advertising copy and, if I found it in any way at all displeasing, to turn it down, which I not infrequently did.

After being thrown out of the financial world, I was promptly welcomed by NBC as a studio page or guide (the customary entry level) at the Rockefeller Center headquarters. The reasoning was that since I had been working in a bank, I knew where the money was for sponsorship. And since I was a musician and lived in close rapport with both union and non-union musicians, I understood this world. Finally, with the law degree I had obtained at night school, they believed I would be able to help defend broadcasters against the predatory practices of the legal profession. This was my second entry-level attempt to find a niche in the business world, but this time I had some cards to play. The duties of a guide were to conduct tours around the NBC studios for out-of-town visitors, but I never actually did a tour. Instead I did what few other guides could do: I played the piano at special events and company parties.

A highlight among these opportunities to entertain occurred in 1939. The World's Fair opened at Flushing Meadows, and a prominent part of the RCA exhibit (RCA was the parent company of NBC) was a public display that was set up to introduce the world to the new medium of television. Of course, there had to be something to watch. A demonstration was set up behind a glass panel, consisting of a studio with a piano, a camera, and a TV receiver. The public could thus watch both a live performance and its reception on a TV set—at the same time. The performance consisted of me playing a musical accompaniment to three comely Powers models, who walked back and forth in a variety of sexy hats and dresses. David Sarnoff, chairman of RCA, was frequently in attendance, observing the technical details and checking out the models. What better way to launch a new art or science or business to the world? The exhibit worked well, I found my niche, and history was made.

A second experimental TV exhibit was set up on the cruise liner *President Roosevelt*, sailing between New York and Bermuda. Following the precedent set at the World's Fair, a similar demonstration was arranged on the deck of the liner, again with myself on piano, the Powers models displaying their assets, and this time also puppet-master Burr Tillstrom in a show of his own creation, which later became a hit on NBC network TV as "Kukla, Fran, and Ollie." The public watched it all on TV sets in the ship's lounge. Bermuda took second place.

Although I was still technically a member of the page and guide staff of NBC, not a single tour did I ever guide through the Rockefeller Center Studios. My duties on the Bermuda run had a most satisfactory ending. It happened that the retired treasurer of RCA lived in Hamilton, Bermuda, and one day he came to see the TV exhibit while we were in port. We struck up an acquaintance. Quite unbeknownst to me, he called David Sarnoff to observe that this young pianist on the TV set seemed to be having too good a time and shouldn't he be given somewhat greater responsibilities? The result was that upon our return to New York, I was made assistant program manager of the NBC Blue Network, one of the two radio networks operated by the company. The world was beginning to make sense. There was music, there were legal problems, there were commercials, all to be stirred into the heady brew of a new enterprise that was full of both promise and chicanery, the two arms of show business. Wall Street had nothing to compare with Toscanini and the NBC Symphony, Fred Waring, Bob Hope, Fred Allen, Dave Garroway, and the other greats of the radio age. Bit by bit, I was becoming involved with them all.

One involvement with the late great Fred Allen I remember with delight. To NBC's leading comic philosopher, life was a battleground on which he, and most of the rest of us, confronted an enemy that he called a vice president. To Fred, "vice president" was a generic term meaning anybody of self-important demeanor who, with temporary corporate backing and title, tried to impose his will on others, particularly in matters of morality, taste, and art, whether it made sense or not.

At that time I was a kind of sword-bearer to the vice president of programming at the network. My duty was to read the script of Fred Allen's next Sunday night show and delete from it any suggestion of indelicacy, double-entendre, sexual eccentricity, moral lapse, or sin in any form whatsoever. I would then return the script to Fred, together with an admonishment that he would be turned off the air if he insisted on delivering the offending lines. This I did in the form of a message from my vice president, who would remain holed up in his concrete cubicle out of communication with the outside world. As it turned out, even there he was not safe from the wrath and scorn of Fred, who in his earthy way championed the rights of ordinary folk to indulge in a wide variety of minor sins as part of their constitutional privilege. For the network, it was a losing battle.

One day Fred brought in a script in which he had as his guest interviewee a falconer, complete with falcon. Nobody worried about this one because it was hard to imagine how a conversation with a falconer could become salacious. A lot of Fred's action scenes were right out of the barnyard, where anything could happen, but falconers are for the great open spaces and the clean fresh air. Thus the falcon, in this case, felt comfortable in the open spaces of NBC's largest studio and took off from his perch, soared around the studio, and dumped on the unprotected heads of the studio audience. Amid general panic, Fred merely observed that the script had been through the usual process of approval and the falcon was simply expressing his views of the script-approval process and those who conduct it.

Fred usually resorted to other media to express his displeasure at the broadcast network's attempts to muzzle him. What was expunged from his radio script would sooner or later appear in print. Anyone with a corporate title was a likely target of his ridicule, but since I had no title at all, he was baffled by the problem of how to get at me. My vice president who let me do his dirty work frequently turned up in the Allen script. Once Fred referred to him by his title in a conversation with Ersil Twing, a character on the Allen show. "What's a vice president?"

asked Ersil. Fred's answer: a vice president is a bit of fungus that becomes attached to the underside of old oaken desks.

"Hmm," went Ersil. "It seems to me there should be some product that could eradicate this fungus."

"There is," replied Fred. "A mysterious Mr. Button goes round from office to office with a long pole with a sponge on the end. This sponge has been dipped in a fungicide, and he sloshes it all over all the desks where vice presidents might be lurking."

"I see," said Ersil, "and is this product our sponsor?"

"Yes," said Fred. "It claims to get rid of vice presidents with one application, or you get your money back."

"Friends," said Ersil, "if you are troubled with low back pain due to a vice president, send us your name and address with a dollar and we will sympathize deeply with you on our way to the bank."

Now this script was declared non grata by the authorities, but two results followed. First, the vice president in charge left NBC shortly afterward. Second, I became known as "the mysterious" Mr. Button, which in a long lifetime, is probably the best title I ever had. All the vice presidents I ever worked for at NBC were in and out of the revolving corporate door, in rapid succession. But as "the mysterious," I escaped notice, censure, and dismissal long enough to have made the friendship of one of the most lovable, considerate, and perceptive public figures in the history of American entertainment. After all, I was really on his side.

◆ ◆ ◆

As I look back on that period, it did not take much of a sense of history to realize that a world war was coming for which nobody seemed to have a plan except maybe Hitler, Hirohito, and Mussolini. There was a sense of something inevitable in which everybody would be involved; but idealism and patriotism, the principles for which people die in wartime, were curiously lacking. Fringe efforts by some antiwar activists and writers, who were warning the public against profiteering by arms merchants, drew some attention. But there was no recruiting for soldiers that I was aware of in these early years, and even if there had been, I was sure I would not have been taken since I was red-green color-blind.

Just getting started in a new job soaked up all my energy and interest. I was learning about expense accounts, perfecting the intricate maneuvers by which program material was created and booked, and enjoying a lively after-hours social life on the glamour circuit. I even wrote some music that found its way to the airwaves. More exorcism than biography, this music was background for a play about a ne'er-do-well piano player who came to a no-good end. The play was aired on the NBC Radio Guild with a fairly good cast. While I as prototype had many opportunities to come to a no-good end, fortunately they remained unfulfilled.

As the drums of war beat abroad, the draft was passed by a slim margin in Congress as soon as our involvement became both inevitable and imminent. As happened to many unmarried, aspiring young men at or near the bottom of the career ladder, the draft board notice came to me, bearing a fairly low number. Indeed, I was the first employee of NBC to be drafted, and while the broadcasting industry might be considered an exempt calling, I did not consider taking advantage of that possibility. In fact, I looked forward to the military experience. It might even take me back to England where I had a sentimental mission in addition to possibly a military one. NBC gave me reasonable assurance of postwar employment, if I returned, and as a parting gift put me on a couple of rigged quiz shows to enhance my salary as a private in the Army. I presently found myself on a train to Fort Dix, New Jersey, together with a hundred other interrupted careerists, one of whom, William McChesney Martin, had been president of the New York Stock Exchange the day before. But we were now all on the same level. Our careers had been taken out of our hands. We had to start new ones. And it did not matter whether I was color-blind. There was work for everyone. As we were to find out before long, the military had just as many, if not more, career opportunities as there were in private business, only this time you bet your life on it and therefore took it seriously. If you did not, you remained a private, with greatly diminished chances of ever coming back. I did come back, however, and it is time to review how, and why, and what took place in the interim.

3
Before the War

MILITARY LIFE BEGAN for me in 1941 at Fort Dix with discipline, drill, and a regular daily schedule for everything. It did not matter that drill sergeants, of barely high-school level, were indoctrinating young professionals and business executives; everyone understood the system, and it was the common objective to make the system work for us, rather than the other way around. We took advantage of the benefits of physical drill. We shined our own boots. We out-saluted the regulars and responded to any order, however meaningless. We were at the bottom of the authority chain, but we were determined to find out how to climb up it, just as we would have if we had still been private citizens instead of private soldiers. The sergeants, whose methods were based on abuse and humiliation, did not understand this. We absorbed all they could dish out. Pretty soon they were, in a sense, working for us.

It did not take the commanding officer long to find out that I was a piano player and a broadcaster. My first special mission in the military was to drive, in the Colonel's car, to the nearest city and purchase a piano for the recreational use of the battalion. In those pre–Pearl Harbor days, entertainment for the troops was at a premium, and I was soon producing weekly amateur shows in addition to my regular drill. Some of these shows revealed enough draftee talent to attract the local radio station, WTAR-Norfolk, the NBC affiliate for that region. Thus I had already embarked on a career synthesis that continued right through the war. For instance, when it came time for the outfit to be sent overseas for real duty, the Colonel, who would not be denied his entertainment, had the piano included in our military materiel in a crate labeled "Machine Guns." Fortunately I did not go with that shipment. The piano ended up in New Guinea.

My battalion went through further training during the course of which I was selected for officer training and in due course emerged as a second lieutenant. We were put in charge of the coastal batteries at Fort Monroe, Virginia, which had been installed to protect the republic against either Confederates or Spaniards, I forget which, but really it did not matter because they did not work anyway. Our real mission was to become an anti-aircraft artillery unit. But the country was so unprepared for war, there was no anti-aircraft artillery equipment for us to train on. We had to go to Great Britain to be trained on theirs. So, in the spring of 1942, orders came for us to proceed to the UK.

An aging tramp steamer of Philippine registry had been drafted into the U.S. Merchant Marine with the assignment of transporting cargo and twelve junior Army officers from Ft. Dix to Glasgow. We were part of the advance guard being sent to Britain to initially strike terror in the breast of Adolf Hitler, should he learn of our presence, and to prepare for the later invasion of Europe. We set sail lightheartedly for Halifax, and from there crossed the Atlantic in a typical convoy of thirty ships guarded by six Canadian Corvettes. It was a time of energetic German submarine activity in the North Atlantic. Ours was a small fleet, but to my eye it used up so much of the visible ocean that I could not imagine a German submarine captain being able to avoid seeing us. Our guards were disciplined and speedy, and we had our own cannon and a ready spirit to repel boarders should there be any.

Two days out of Halifax, somewhere off Iceland, the steering gear of our freighter ceased functioning. In keeping with the rules, the convoy sailed on without us, the signaling lamps of the other ships bidding us farewell. A friendly fog settled over us, and we drifted around between Greenland and Iceland while the engineer tinkered with the machinery, alternately kicking it and cursing it in Tagalog dialect. We passengers relaxed on the after-deck, eating doughnuts and scanning the sea for periscopes.

Soon the crew had the ship going again properly, but the captain made no effort to catch up to the convoy because he was an independently minded man and did not take kindly to discipline in any form. As a result, we cruised into the Firth of Forth about two weeks late, but alive and well. In the meantime, word was passed around that our ship was missing, and presumed sunk. Ships passing by Iceland were advised to look out for survivors. Debris was indeed sighted. Search planes made futile flights to and from Reykjavik. We soon passed from the category of gallant lost cause to that of a confounded nuisance to those who were supposed to find us.

The Army, which takes care of its own, concluded that since nobody had buried us at sea, those safely ashore in Scotland should do the next best thing, namely bury us, figuratively speaking, on land. This they proceeded to do. A memorial service was put in motion, complete with flags at half-mast, buglers with puckered lips, chaplains in cassocks, and somber music from an antique pump organ attempting to enhance the solemnity of the occasion with pious wheezes and groans. A hymn was sung in spite of this. Into this solemn scene there intruded a six-by-six Army truck bearing the twelve missing officers, presumed dead but obviously very much alive. They filed into the back row without disrupting the service. The chaplain read the names of the hitherto absentees. At the last name, the funereal silence was shattered by a brisk "All present and accounted for."

Now the Army has no manual on resurrections: the chaplaincy normally does that kind of service but once a year at Easter. However, everyone was delighted at the turn of events—everyone, that is, except the clerks who had to reverse all the paperwork that normally accompanies corpses or disappearances. The twelve officers, reinstated in their proper stations, resumed their military lives. They had been granted a second chance.

From my first days as a draftee, I was aware that this might be a one-way journey. Therefore, I thought it my duty to my parents to render as full an account as the censors would allow of how my time was spent away from home. This I did in my letters addressed to M. & P., which they saved, perhaps also expecting the worst. The following selection of excerpted letters traces my humble activities as a recruit until I crossed the Atlantic and arrived in Northern Ireland. For easier reading, I have dispensed with the salutation and closing remarks after the first letter.

❖ ❖ ❖

Sunday, April 1941
Battery A. 14th Battalion, Ft. Eustis, Virginia
Dear M. & P.,

THIS IS HOW we live. There's a long white building, two stories high, in a row of other long white buildings along a street. Each floor is a dormitory with fourteen beds on each side, and toilet at the end. At the head of each bed is a trunk, and at the foot, a chair.... That is "home."

At five of six, we are wakened, dress, line up outside, are accounted for, and then have breakfast at 6:30 AM. And a very good breakfast, I'll swear to that before anybody. French toast, eggs, cereals, sausages, bacon—I've worked in the kitchen and it's prepared as well as it's humanly possible to prepare food for such a crowd. After breakfast, we are either drilled or we do day labor, one one day, one the next. The sergeants give orders to the corporals, who then tell us to work when the officers are around but not otherwise. Since we are in a new camp, there is much ditch digging and gardening to do, and as yet we have had nothing more military than ordinary marching forward, backward, sideways or all three at once. Work finishes at 4:30 PM and from then on we are on our own. There are personal things to be done, shoes shined, etc. and between 4:30 and 9:30 the time flies. Lights go out at 9:30 PM. Some of the soldiers do too. I am usually asleep by 9:15 and so far the life has done me very well.

We have weekends free and I shall use one of them to visit Washington. New York is a little too far for a weekend trip. But Virginia Beach isn't so far away, so why don't you run down for a long weekend spring vacation?

I haven't seen W. Martin since the first day but my company is at least interesting. Two Chinese, an Austrian and a French refugee, several Brooklyn and Bronx city types and a group of farm boys from the Middle West.

We are here for thirteen weeks to get basic training in harbor defense, which is all right with me: our front lawn is decorated with four large pieces of antique field artillery which we must learn to fire, but personally I can't imagine coast artillery in this country assuming a very important place in whatever is coming.

Would you send me some underwear and a few pairs of white socks. I will have Miss Wickens take care of that wedding present. Other than that, everything seems to be in order and I am getting a good rest. What news?

Love to all,
Private Button

❖   ❖   ❖

Sunday, May 1941

OUR LATEST TOY, now that we've learned how to destroy people with gas and airplanes, is what's known as a 155-millimeter cannon that shoots a shell weighing 100 lbs twelve miles. The entire gun weighs eighteen tons and takes thirteen men to operate. We form crews of thirteen each, and practice the routine of loading and firing, all of which has to be done in the impossible time of twenty seconds. The barrel recoils six feet and the idea is not to get in the way of it. This is no job for a pianist.

One nice thing about this is that we keep getting new clothes. Just got part of our summer equipment, and it's perfectly good stuff for anybody. They are teaching us how to roll packs in preparation for some big maneuvers in the near future. And we have to pack them up, put them on, march down the road, pitch our tents, pack up and march back again for practice. That sounds like hot work in the state of Virginia but the truth is I haven't discarded the Long Johns since I joined the Army. This is a cold peninsula we're on and the nights are like Eagle's Mere [lakeside community in Pennsylvania]. The days are clear and cool, like autumn. And there doesn't seem to be any spring at all.

Some of our classes now are in the use of complicated, trigonometric devices called plotting boards—having to do with the way a shell travels thru the air—the speed, wind, earth curve, and other obscure factors that put you off your target. The boys on the plotting board in action work under the protection of six feet of steel and concrete, as they are the brains of an artillery room. Much as I dislike arithmetic I suppose I shall have to learn it again and be a plotter. The artillery room seems like a safe place to be during any real action.

❖ ❖ ❖

Sunday, June 16, 1941

WELL THIS LIFE is much like NBC in some ways. We decide to do a show and I, with another private, organize the thing and produce it. I act as master of ceremonies and play in the band too, and it works out to be a great success, the talent all consisting of lowly but gifted privates with a full military routine all day long for just $21 a month. Just like the pages and guides at NBC.

To be modest about it, our show went off excellently and we had fun doing it. It was scheduled for 8 PM Friday night, and the General had been invited and accepted—a great honor for us. He arrived at 7:59, and the hall was already overflowing. Everyone jumped to attention, and silence, while he and a flock of colonels, captains etc. took their seats. The orchestra was already on the stage—we had no curtain. They smacked a chord and I walked out and started according to studied instructions about proper sequence—"General Nichols, Officers, Ladies and men of the 14th Battalion, welcome to the first edition, etc., etc." The audience had to be addressed in that order.

Our first number, a real eye-opener, was a special arrangement of "Amapola." We had three trumpets, three trombones, three saxes and four rhythm, with an arranger formerly with the big bands in N.Y. and a very well coordinated unit. All of them except one sax and myself were regular members of the military band and used to playing loud. That was what the soldiers wanted, I guess, because they whistled and screamed and raised the roof. It was the first live entertainment they had seen since April.

Next was a tap dancer, the regular nightclub type and fairly good. He was encored. Then came a vocal swing quartet put together by one of a very well-known radio troupe called the "Kidoodlers." Next, another orchestra number called "Britches" with a vocalist. Before we knew it everybody in the audience was singing with us. They ate it up.

Then for contrast, which Mr. Wade at NBC would have insisted, we had a "raconteur" with musical accompaniment. This was a sophisticated smooth sort of act and still got the same response. Next a singer of things like "Melancholy Baby" who got the crowd singing with him on his last choruses.

In between these acts, while I would be making an introduction, we had two stooges who came on and just walked across the stage, regardless of what was going on, usually they had one punch line which was slightly risqué and which brought down the house. We used them to kid the officers or play up camp situations—inside humor, you'd call it.

After the singer, another tap and then an act like a Chamber Music Society in which the drummer played on three tin cans nailed to a board making such a din that he stole the entire show. They wouldn't let the ensemble go. I finally said they'd be back, and meanwhile we'd go on with the show. Next came a suave Spanish guitarist who couldn't read a note but who on one eight-string guitar managed to sound like an entire rumba rhythm section. We found that the Colonel's wife was Spanish, so we dedicated his selections to her, and she was delighted.

After that a sketch, blackout fashion, and then we had a singer named Darnell, from Bob Chester's orchestra, who sang "Stardust" and "My Sister and I" just as he recorded them, and again the crowd tore the roof off. Then a brilliant dancer called Valerian Matuszeskie, a real professional. Then a finale, which began with the "General Nichols March," especially composed by the orchestra leader with a parade of eight men representing the evolution of a soldier. When they were all on, we did a glee club number about Fort Eustis; then the band went into the "Star Spangled Banner" and the show ended. But no sooner were the brass hats out of sight than the band took off into the "South Rampart Street Parade" and let go with six brass going full speed. Nobody could bugle the camp to bed because the bugler was up on the stage playing hot rides on his trumpet and not caring a hang about taps.

Official comment on Saturday was highly favorable and everybody was astounded at the finish of the show. Heretofore most of the shows have been slapstick, smutty burlesque skits, and people suspected this would be just another. But the impression on Saturday was that the sooner we give another show the better. It was a great experience and the volume of response was very satisfying.

We were supervised by the Morale Officer, a Lt. Adams from Alabama, who much prefers boogie-woogie piano to soldiering. He was chief arranger and music director of Columbia's Richmond station and we gab about arrangements by the hour. Yesterday he, his wife and I got in the car, went to Richmond, saw a show, and had a big dinner, saw some of Civil War Richmond and then came back about 11 P.M. Today I have done nothing at all.

Please send me a pair of summer pajamas.

June 1941

TWO WEEKS AGO we started in on a course called "Orientation." It developed into a comprehensive study of civil engineering, complete with transit, field notes, shooting the sun, observing Polaris and all manner of higher mathematics with Greek letters instead of numbers. I became thoroughly confused and worried. Some of these men are ex-engineers and very much at home in the subject; to others including me, it was Greek in more ways than one. You can imagine my surprise when an instructor told me I had scored 91 and 95 in the two parts of the exam.

For the past four Sundays I have been organist at the school church, and we have a choir of some twenty voices. I play preludes and postludes and hymns and interludes and have a wonderful time. The chapel has a new Hammond.

Last week our course was in seacoast gunner problems; this week in machine guns; next week some minor subjects and we are through. If you plan to come over on the 4th there are some things I'll need: a steamer trunk, for instance—one of our camp trunks will do. And send me a blank to renew my NJ auto license please.

No word as to our destination yet.

August 21, 1941

MY OFFICIAL STATUS is now that of acting corporal, which is corporalhood in every sense but that of salary. I am addressable as corporal, wear two chevrons and to the world I am Corporal R. E. Button, but on the books I am Pfc Button, and that is some increase in $ over private but I haven't yet been able to figure out what. Corporal gets $54 a month; I am somewhere between $36 and $54.

The commanding General of the 1st Army, soon to go on full field maneuvers in North Carolina, called up General Nichols of Ft. Eustis and requested that I be detached to the Public Relations staff of the 1st Army for maneuvers. Public relations work involves radio, newspaper and movie coverage of the maneuvers. Col. Hafer called up the General of Ft. Eustis to try to get the whole move cancelled, as he needed my services here, but the General prevailed and my reputation did not suffer by the competition between colonels and generals for my services.

This whole thing is an outcome of my visit to Washington. There at the War Department they said I could go out on maneuvers as sort of a breaking-in; then if I did a good job, maybe return permanently to Washington. If I did not go back to Washington, the Col. had already promised to recommend me to officers' school after my first six months service (the minimum). School is three months. Then you become a 2nd Lieutenant ($125 a month).

Here at Ft. Eustis we have developed a troupe of entertainers that we use at Rotary Club dinners and the like. Music, jokes etc. Last night at the monthly dinner of Newport News Rotary Club, I gave a talk on the Army, NBC and life in general. It was very well received. At the end of the meeting, they wanted to sing "God Bless America" and for a moment I couldn't remember how it started. So I played a chord in F, and one of the Rotarians began to sing and I suddenly remembered everything!

We play every Thursday night for dances here and every Friday night at Langley Field. Our new recruits are due in this Saturday.

❖   ❖   ❖

December 1941 [after Pearl Harbor]

SINCE MY LAST letter was a pre-war one, I have to revise it a bit. We are now restricted to the post and can't get off for any reason short of a complete personal emergency. Thus furloughs are automatically cancelled until further notice. There is a chance of a very short leave around Christmas but no definite orders have been issued as yet. All we have been told is to be prepared to leave here on two hours notice for duty elsewhere. In view of that I will probably send home some books and civilian clothes and other junk that I hope you will keep intact. One has to travel light. My only problem is to find boxes and string and the other stuff that is usually so easily located in the kitchen drawer.

The interview with the Officer Candidate's Board consisted of two questions. I approached and saluted, was given "at ease" and the boss officer asked, "How old are you?" to which I made proper reply—twenty-six. Then the officers thumbed through my application grunting to each other. After they had sniffed at the record for a few more minutes one looked up and said again, "How old did you say you were?" I answered and another officer said, "He works for the NBC." More grunts and I was dismissed. Today as I was passing Battalion Headquarters, an officer stopped me to say, "In case you hadn't heard, you did very well before the Board yesterday." This you realize is entirely a Ft. Eustis operation—that is to say, it is not a political job, but one based on my record here speaking for itself. Just like NBC.

The general reaction of the fellows here over the outbreak of war is a feeling of concern at the failure of the defenses of Hawaii to function any better, especially after all the ballyhoo about how strong they were. Otherwise there is an absence of surprise and a general eagerness to come to grips with the real problem instead of fooling around the way we do in a Replacement Center. There is general acceptance of the fact that the Coast Artillery and Anti-Aircraft Artillery branches will see the soonest action after the Navy and it is likely to be anywhere in the world. But nobody complains and as a matter of fact I bet the atmosphere here is a lot more calm than it is in the civilian world with its extra editions and excited rumors. We don't care about rumors because we have to take orders regardless; the civilian does not get his mind made up for him and is more likely to listen to all the wild nonsense that is bound to develop in the first few weeks of war. I hope you are not upset or alarmed and too excited to make some more of those cookies.

❖   ❖   ❖

March, 1942, At Sea [on route to Halifax, Nova Scotia]

LAST NIGHT, AFTER a pleasant day's sail, we ran into a cold, thick fog. In no time at all the bow of the ship was practically out of sight and all that remained of our convoy was a series of foghorn blasts. The Captain got set on what he considered to be the right course, and when the other foghorns began getting fainter he declared that the convoy was getting lost, not himself. He is an amiable but violent sort of person, a Filipino, who has already dodged fifty-four Jap bombers and some Jap subs. Well, very soon the night and fog closed over us like a tent and with them a complete silence. At that point the radio brought in the hardly comforting news that considerable sub activity was reported in this area. (Earlier in the afternoon our escort had let go two depth charges but we didn't see anything.) I was due to go on watch at 4:00 AM so there was nothing to do but go to bed and leave everything in the hands of God, the skipper and our six lookouts, which is precisely what we all did.

Sure enough, at 3:30 in the morning we were still nosing along at slow speed, the fog just as thick on the water, but overhead the sky had cleared and the stars were all out. I went up to the bridge to find that although we hadn't heard any other ships, the skipper knew where we were. We weren't lost, yet he cussed all the other captains for not being right around us. It was good and cold out there. I had on two pairs of woolen underwear, two pairs socks, shoes and arctics, shirt, jacket, overcoat, life-preserver, knit hat, winder cap, helmet and gloves. Added to that, when on watch one wears a telephone set connected with all the other lookouts. I never saw a morning that looked so good. The sun chased the fog away and the ocean turned clear blue, and we all shot off a few rounds from our guns just for a test.

✦ ✦ ✦

May 12, 1942

WE HAVE ANCHORED in what the newspapers furtively refer to as "an Eastern Canadian port," and for all I know brother Donny may be in one of the many planes that circle around all the time overhead. It certainly is good to be in a cozy land-locked harbor within sight of things like trains, buses, dogs and houses. It isn't even Spring here yet.

✦ ✦ ✦

May 23, 1942

AFTER A FEW false starts it seems to be about time for our ocean cruise. Meanwhile we have gotten slightly acquainted with Halifax and after the natives were assured that the U.S. hadn't invaded the country, they uniformly expressed the opinion that it would be a good thing if the U.S. did take over Canada. What with the French Canadians balking at draft rules, and the Maritime Provinces rebelling at the unequal gas ration, Canadians aren't too happy or pleased with their government.

I had a seven-dollar conversation with Donny in lieu of a visit. Our times off didn't fit but we had a fine telephonic reunion. I almost bummed a ride down on a bomber but the return trip was in doubt so the Capt. withheld his permission for the trip.

To pass the time we have classes, a few dates, a movie, and target practice offshore with the Canadian Navy. Yesterday I shot down a small balloon at some four hundred yards up and away, using a Lewis automatic rifle—the kind gangsters use in the movies. Hope German planes are as easy.

No mail is coming thru to us, and it probably won't till we land somewhere. I wish I could see that ring on my fiancée, or rather, Janet with the ring on. Take some pictures of her. I hope she doesn't get lonesome.

Every time I put on my tan shirt I reflect on where I got its last pressing, which was in our kitchen. That was the most lasting impression the shirt ever received.

Must run along—it looks like the best defense we might have for a while is the good old Newfoundland Grand Banks pea-soup fog.

4

Northern Ireland

AFTER OUR LATE arrival at Glasgow, I was quickly dispatched to Northern Ireland where I presently found myself in a beautiful, verdant field in County Down amongst cows, leprechauns and elements of the British Army. Here was to begin our training in the martial arts. What better place to learn how to kill people, shoot down aircraft, pull the lanyard of a cannon, mow down hordes of Hessians with a machine gun, and generally strike terror into the heart of the enemy, and have it all stop for tea promptly at 4 o'clock. After that would come parties with the natives, featuring British country dancing, Irish jigs, and Yankee swing. But then, the BBC evening news would remind us of bombings, sinkings, Nazi and Japanese successes, and turbulence in our homeland. It was a case of making the most of each day, for we all knew, but did not talk much about, where we were headed and into what danger.

The regiment was billeted on the property of a landed-gentry family named Hart. They possessed a long history including the ancestral Doe Castle (now on the National Trust), a comely daughter named Marion, and a good grand piano. It was on the Hart family piano that I learned to play the Warsaw Concerto, which became a staple of my public performing ever since. The war remained in the background while I conducted a thorough research project on all three of these family icons. The only military incident that occurred during that period was when my anti-aircraft gunners by mistake shot down a fat sausage-shaped barrage balloon that was hanging in the sky protecting Londonderry Naval Base. This caused the British to conclude that they had as much to fear from the Americans as from the Germans, but since the German Air Force never showed up that far north, the whole incident was resolved with apologies and some bourbon whiskey.

Meanwhile Marion Hart's brother, George, an RAF pilot, flew to America for training, and visited Maplewood, N.J. which ultimately led to his marriage to my sister Anne. This almost included a reciprocal romance between myself and Marion, but fate decided otherwise. Marion could not carry a tune. Nevertheless, as a gesture of goodwill, she got herself assigned to the Women's Royal Naval Service in London just in time to greet me as I arrived there from Northern Ireland. Her presence greatly facilitated my transition from relative peace in Ireland to a new assignment in London. But this time, Marion receded into the background, and I finally became involved in the war, along with several million Londoners, who had for three years been standing alone against the Germans and who were jolly glad to see the Yanks arriving, even though we were "oversexed, overpaid, and over here."

◆ ◆ ◆

Letters home from this time reveal the almost bucolic and strangely incongruous nature of my first six months of war service in the UK. As one would expect, my first dispatch was such a detailed account of our crossing that the censors had to work overtime.

◆ ◆ ◆

June 16, 1942, Ireland

I'LL ASSUME THAT there is a general exchange of news and that you may have heard some details of the trip and the new location. Mail here is very eccentric in delivery but I have some dated May 29th, which is quite prompt for this place. Airmail seems to come through very well.

You'd think that the Army and Navy between them would have kept track of our little advance detachment (twelve officers and seven sergeants) but no; the regiment landed in Scotland some two weeks ahead of us so that we became the rear guard instead; they took six days to [censored] five weeks all told, and the Army headquarters didn't know where we were for the last three. [censored] had to have a new "de-Gaussing" or de-magnetizing, on the ship, to prevent action by magnetic mines. Then we sat in [censored] for a while, goodness knows why; then one fine day in [censored] when we were moving out to sea, the pilot ordered starboard and the ship turned to port, and down went the anchor for another week while we had repairs and waited for the next convoy. No word of this reached the Regiment. Finally we took off and spent a lot of time in dense fog, which meant slow speed for days. Once out in the middle the rudder broke again, electrical contacts or some such detail, and since the convoy passed on without us, we all prepared for an attack. This was somewhere about the longitude of [censored]. Soon the defect was fixed and we caught up. By this time the Colonel, in Scotland, couldn't find out anything about us from the Navy except a vague report that we had landed on [censored] in lifeboats. So he tried to arrange for some planes to pick us up there but the report turned out to be false. Then the Regiment started thinking about having a memorial service for us! And all the time we were stuffing with excellent food, and generally enjoying ourselves signaling back and forth with the other ships.

Scotland finally loomed up and we passed right by it into the Firth of [censored] which is a beautiful passage. Industry on one side, farms on the other, and the river sometimes gets as narrow as that river in [censored] that you pass over on the train. Yet they launched the *Queen Mary* there. We landed in Glasgow and spent [censored] while the Army was made to understand that we were still alive. Then another [censored] trip to Belfast, and we caught up to the rest at a camp on a sort of point or peninsula jutting out in the Irish Sea, an unbelievable, postcard-picture kind of place, with a neat little light-house, clean, well-arranged farms all around and a tremendous mountain (Slieve Donard, Mourne Mts.) as background. We are just out in a field, in tents, being trained by the British. This of course means daily tea, war or no war, and rugby games after dinner, or sometimes we teach them our baseball or football. It's very pleasant. There are woman soldiers to do the clerical work, K.P. and act as waitresses, but some even man the guns. In theory, we don't have anything to do with them socially, but it is a pleasant change to have them around. It seems to be the usual thing in the British Army, and I hear the U.S. is starting the same business on a voluntary basis.

Our weekly day off is Friday, so that the men can go into Belfast and shop. Sunday we work as usual with the exception of church at 8:00 AM, and in that I take the usual post at the organ. It's the foot pump type and calls for great concentration. The hymns luckily are all familiar, so I can concentrate on my feet.

I am learning to live very simply and have about everything I need, except for candy. We can buy three bars of chocolate a week (five-cent bars). Would you give the Maplewood paper my correct address, which now is A.P.O 813, N.Y.C, so I can get that? Incidentally, I have never been in better condition or fatter than I am now, (not fat, but muscle) and Hitler, I am told, has become badly frightened by this news.

◆ ◆ ◆

July 27, 1942

THIS AFTERNOON I happened to be working on certain projects at a certain place when one of those present invited me to fly over to England for dinner. Without believing that he was serious I indicated that nothing would be more pleasant or more improbable, to my mind, and before I knew it I was in the top turret of a Wellington bomber, easing gently over first Ulster, then the Irish Sea, the Isle of Man, bits of Wales and finally a town in Shropshire, near Shrewsbury.

There we sat down to a wonderful meal in the RAF Officers Mess, chatted a bit and then headed into the sunset over Ireland again. It was a perfectly beautiful summer day, with little woolly clouds and a clear blue ocean and, just as we came in, a large full moon peeking over the horizon. Although Germans were around West England (according to the radio) we saw none. But all the guns were loaded. We were dressed up in "Mae West" jackets—sort of a life preserver with so many safety gadgets on it you end up being completely unsafe from the confusion of trying to remember which cord does what and where. Look up St. John's Point on the map—that was where we headed across the sea. Also notice the Mountains of Mourne—just south—which I have climbed many times.

As a result of a tea I attended and played at, word got around that the Americans had a pianist with them. The hospital called up and asked if I would play on a program for the convalescents. A Miss Spaulding, from Boston, runs the Hospital's activities of this type. We arranged a program last Thursday and had an audience of some three hundred bathrobed and pajamaed soldiers. There was a soloist, a reader and I, rather informally. I asked what they wanted to hear. Luckily one man insisted on the "Rachmaninoff G Minor", another the "Rhapsody in Blue," and then some recent popular tunes. Of course such an audience spoils a person; you really think you are a good player from the amount of applause. I thoroughly enjoyed myself and had a pretty good piano with easy key action and plenty of fortissimo so like any ham I made lots of noise and played everything as fast as I possibly could. They liked it.

The reader on the program was Lady Avril Anderson, daughter of the one-time Mayor of Derry, Sir Charles Anderson, and one of her activities was the management of the weekly Sunday evening hour for the services at the Derry Methodist Church. Inevitably I found myself playing there Sunday night, to about two hundred soldiers, sailors and RAF personnel. They were even better than the hospital. And when for encores I started playing medleys of Victor Herbert, etc. they wouldn't let it stop and the concert, which is supposed to run from 8 to 9:30, ran on in this manner till quarter to eleven.

This experience made me recall Washington's offer back in May and it rather justified the decision I made then. This was the most tangible morale job I have ever done. Here were a crown of minesweeper crews and plane pilots and sub sailors all living on borrowed time, so to speak, and it became my privilege to dispense something that seemed very valuable to them and which to me was pure enjoyment and relaxation. It hardly seemed right to be thanked for doing it.

Walking back from the church we passed the county house of the Lyle family, and on inquiry I found not only that the Lyles are numerous in Londonderry County but that they are one of the old and original "county" families. There are George Lyles, Hugh Lyle, Samuel Lyle, Sydney Lyle and one Colonel Lyle of Knocktarns. Send me some dope on our family connections with Lyles and I'll go into their histories here (discreetly).

Last week I drove down to Carrickfergus near Belfast and returned along the absolutely fantastic Antrim coast. There for centuries the O'Neills have been making trouble, killing each other when no McQuillans were in sight or no Englishman, and all the cliffs still contain towers, castles, abutments, and devices to repel a Viking invasion. The scenery is magnificent until you come to Portrush, where people go for holidays, and it is a miniature Atlantic City. We stopped at the Giants Causeway, which is anything but gigantic, but is an interesting rock formation. For some reason the British associate even natural phenomena with tea—you go to the Giant's Causeway as much for tea as for wonderment.

Every other week we have a dance with the forty-odd American nurses down the road, and it is a wonderful party—partly because there are just enough to go around and the poor girls get tired of their doctor-colleagues. Saturday nights the Officers Club has a function that we attend, usually with a supper party first. Suppers are arranged by the local dowagers; one has been at a beautiful old sixteenth-century place called Ballynagaard House (a Colonel Hart and family), another at Ballyharnet House (Sir Dudley McCorkell, local squire), another at Deanfield House, where Lady Anderson lives. They are a fine lot of people, and much less spoiled than the British. And very proud. And basically loyal but composed of very obscure but nonetheless vigorous political notions. They seem to enjoy our company. Of course, these manor houses all have good pianos, sometimes weighted down with bric-a-brac collected from somebody's travels in India or Africa and a gilded saddle blanket from some general's equipage but once you shove back the relics and open the piano, it turns out to be a beauty.

Across the street there is one of those manor houses, but the military has moved in and the sons and daughter are in the services elsewhere. The father is dead and there remains Miss Morisson, the English governess, who speaks six languages including Russian and serves an excellent tea. We call her "Morrie" and she is quite continental, polished and sophisticated. She is a Wagner-phile and we have some interesting musical bull-sessions (tho she'd never call them that). She brought up the whole family, and is flawlessly polished in manners. I chop wood for her fireplace when I feel like exercise, and I am learning the "Moonlight Sonata" (per Hospital request) on her excellent grand piano. She has moved to a building on the estate that is much like our family hideaway in Bucks County.

Our Colonel has told me that because he is pleased with my military performance he is putting thru my 1st Lieutenant papers as of Aug 1; it will be a few weeks coming thru. This being the first promotion amongst the 2nd Lts., I thereby become senior and first in line for the next captaincy.

About Col. Arter. He is public relations man in Belfast—actually no direct connection to us and he doesn't know me. I'm not in p.r. work. I'm still a Regimental functionary, supposedly fighting a war. Haven't had time to approach the public relations crowd yet but they are the proper contact for this broadcast business which I could do any time I can get to Belfast on Sunday. I am carrying a large responsibility in the regiment and have avoided so far getting into that circle, because if the war is to be won more people have to do the dirty work and fewer try to wangle screwy jobs like public relations. I now feel I'll be back sooner if I stick to the war—if it ever opens up. We are the first ones to land on beaches.

❖   ❖   ❖

August 15, 1942

Nowadays it's not only cold—it's perpetually rainy as well. But like all islands, you can go to a hilltop where miles of countryside will be visible and you can see a small rain squall in one area, a few patches of sunshine elsewhere, and mountains of all different colors at once, from the various little "pieces" of weather over them.

From this perspective I have had plenty of chance to think about home. My sentiments are partly regret at the poor use I made of home, and partly wonderment that you two have survived the unhappy complications of raising four kids. Of course the times we lived in were particularly hard on home life, and financial confusion didn't help, but the more I think about it the more apparent it becomes that the fundamentals of a steady home have not changed from the times of Alexander the Great to now. If eternal vigilance buys peace for a nation, it does even more so for a home and family. It seems as if the whole effort of our business world were directed toward breaking up the family—the kinds of products we are urged to buy, the kind of places large numbers of people must live in, the pressure to attend passive entertainments and the pandering to the less respectable motives—all these things seem to my mind to be aimed at the unwary, i.e. the majority of people, and to be decorated with the false sanction of "modernity" while they really serve as the means for the smarter people to climb up over the others.

So, what is there left? The greatest thoughts of other generations do not change and are easily had; the outdoors puts on the greatest shows in the world, and you can't hurry the growth of a person's mind and soul any more than you can force the grass to grow faster. All you can do is give it the proper food, and something inexplicable happens. And the grass will continue to grow under Republicans, Democrats, Fascists, Socialists or the next as yet unheard of political theory which will probably blossom forth, complete with a leader, from the upper reaches of the Amazon River.

However, much as I miss home in the family sense, I can't imagine what it would be like to return to the U.S. now—it just couldn't be. What would the country do with us? Before the war there wasn't even enough motivation in the economic system to call forth everyone's energies and there has been no basic change in our system yet. And since our present objective seems to be the obliteration of one nation of 70 million and another of 90 million, how long will that take? Obviously we are to spend the rest of our days doing it, or policing the job after it is done, and if it is done right, the Anglo-U.S. Empire will stretch right around the world except for Russia. We cannot stop short of that now. And we can't come home. If we did we couldn't go on about our business in the old ways. People have tested the inspiration of a larger motive—however vague it may be—than that of selling more trinkets, or thinking up new descriptions of the tired old luxuries—and I shouldn't think that anyone would want to go back. Certainly fighter pilots will never want to become salesmen, and ski-troopers won't want to return to clerking, and destroyer skippers won't much take to ferryboats. And people who have faced a common danger in the same frame of mind will not be satisfied with the petty competition and polite throat-cutting of our system of "private enterprise."

That's enough philosophizing for one morning, don't you think? It all started and ends with the fact that I miss home.

✦ ✦ ✦

September 20, 1942

I DON'T KNOW what the Colonel is trying to make me into, but I am now Regimental financial agent, member of the court-martial, umpire for certain maneuvers and general liaison officer between the Regiment and the neighboring civilians. It doesn't add up to a great amount of work. I can still chop Miss Morrison's logs and practise a bit on her piano. She is also a linguist, so we practise a bit of German sometimes in the evening.

Some of our number seem to feel that the only wounds the 209th will ever get will be from cutting their lips on the edge of a teacup. I don't know what the generals are waiting for but from my experience so far it's probably the various headquarters trying to decide what time tea will be served, and who gets carbon copies of the invitations. And I think we are going to be the tail end of an invasion when it does pop—what with the band and all, we will set up in the Berlin *tier-garten* and play to soothe the populace. Jerry's infantry outfit should, I think, be almost the first to go over the top. We're way behind them.

Day by day I train communications crews, run around the countryside laying wire and setting up telephone systems—it's all good fun and excellent exercise. Then too I have an amazing collection of RCA gadgets, which can practically hear the birds singing in Berlin and tell you at what height they are flying. Technically the junk is somewhat beyond me but I have a good staff of sergeants and corporals who were radio hams back home and can handle almost anything in that line.

✦ ✦ ✦

October 6, 1942, Lurgan, N. Ireland

THE PICTURE HERE has changed somewhat. Army HQ in London, because of the vast members of troops arriving, ordered the formation of a new M.P. Company, which is to have the job of military police for all North Ireland. On Friday I was forthwith transferred to this company, and am second in command. Later the same day, I was placed in charge of the M.P. detachment at General Hartle's HQ, on my own, with forty-four men to organize, train and run what should be the crack M.P. outfit in Ireland. With the supervision of three large towns forty miles apart we have duties of making felicitous connections with the public police, inspection, hotel owners, churches, etc. General Hartle is known as "Scrappy," and he exercises direct supervision over his M.P.s. This in three days has been a more stimulating military experience than six months in the 209th.

Here I get up at 7:00 AM, go to breakfast at the Castle and then do various errands, like mail censoring, official bulletins, etc. till 10, when I inspect the platoon. Our schedule runs thus: 10 AM reveille, drill and calisthenics and field hiking till 11:30, lunch, class in some topic from one to 3 PM, outdoor stuff 3-4, supper 4:30, guard and patrolling till midnight, except that one set of posts must be guarded twenty-four hours daily. I actually conduct the AM drill and classes, with help from lecturers from various special sections. In the evenings either I study for a class, or go to the Brownlow Arms Hotel bar and pass the evening with the Colonels, Majors, Captains and Kings—they drinking, I playing and listening to the gossip and various overtones. My sergeant calls me there if there is any serious trouble with the patrols.

The captain comes down from Belfast now and then, asks a few questions and returns, so that actually there is no one to tell me how to do things, and only a bunch of fuss-budgety old officers here to say yes to, and my direct superiors here on the staff are excellent to work for.

All I want for Christmas is a description of how the house looks, and what you have for dinner, and how the candlelight service was, and what effect the winter air has on Janet's cheeks.

❖ ❖ ❖

October 12, 1942, N. Ireland

YOU WILL PROBABLY, and rightly, ask how the h—l I expect to win a war for the U.S. by playing the piano, or playing anything else, for that matter, but actually there developed a situation in Derry where there was little else to do but drink or raise a breed of one's favorite type of domestic live-stock, or both, so if my last letters have given you the impression that I was not whole-heartedly going about the business of learning war, you must not think that, and one reason for my feeling misfit was the fact that our real business in Europe seemed to have become the very last thing in the Regiment's collective mind.

What has happened now you might compare to Strauss' "Death and Transfiguration." It has been somewhat like leaving the Guaranty Trust and starting with NBC. I am the sole officer for forty-four "good men and true," upon whose appearance and performance everyone from General Hartle down has already expressed compliment. I censor all their mail, of course, and I find that they like their work, their officer, and their surroundings. I am responsible for their health, morale, training in courtesy, jui jitsu, mob psychology, military law, first aid, and other subjects, and this means that before I can give them a class in anything I must study it on a ration of three hours study to about one hour's class, which keeps me very busy.

The men are proud of their work and have made friends of the soldiers we deal with. We are responsible for order in three towns. One town has Negro troops and here are all the problems of mixed races, but they are worked out by a mixed board of white and black sergeants along the lines which would make an excellent procedure for U.S.A itself. I work closely with the various District Inspectors of the Royal

Ulster Constabulary, these being the selected, most-educated and younger people in Ireland and the least bigoted. I encounter every problem that a soldier in a military area ever meets—from drunkenness and concubines to lost belongings and personal records—and I really feel like a combination sleuth and Sunday School teacher. I have encountered the old situation of a local pub where generals and colonels gather in droves. There being a good piano there, I play almost nightly song-fests, and have the interesting opportunity of observing conduct in high places which sometimes is not favorably comparable with that of soldiers.

✦ ✦ ✦

October 17, 1942

IF JANET READS you my last letter to her you will understand what I mean by the G-2 Section. The fact that I traveled around Germany and got into an *Arbeitsdienst-lage* [German youth camp] is enough to give me a chance at courses conducted in Cambridge now for intelligence officers—"refresher" courses in German, things military, etc.—all things that Uncle Mort Easton could give you the low-down on. I have been studying my German for a few weeks now to get back into the swing of it. And should I have to go back to the 209th the present, the London possibility remains hot, and the G-2 warm.

In Cookstown, one of my assignments, lives the family of Harold Woolesley, the District Inspector of the Royal Ulster Constabulary. There is Harold, about twenty-seven, his sister Dorothy, and his M. & P., the father a retired linen manufacturer. Last evening the ladies of Cookstown threw a dance, and I took Dorothy, or rather Harold and I took Dorothy. It was the nicest party I've been to in Ireland. Mostly British, a typical Woman's Club function, with most of the women in evening gowns and fur wraps, even some tuxedos and tails—very rare for war-time functions.

Saturday nights in a Lurgan blackout are rare experiences. Hundreds of people out just walking around the streets, no cars to speak of, a din of conversation, girls squealing and soldiers laughing, odd accents all around from invisible persons. On one corner a Salvation Army band conducting a hymn-sing and on the next a rip-roaring dance hall which I periodically inspect. As you walk up and down the streets you bump into every age and variety of person—and I mean actually bump into them. Then wander over to the Brownlow Arms and ring the bell thrice—the signal, or else nobody lets you in—and go in for a Guinness and a song or two. Goodness knows how the hotel makes any money. It is run by three pretty Irish girls (Sheila, Roisin and Molly McCaffery) who are very nice people, and very capable of standing off elderly Colonels. The Hotel looks and is run like a comic strip conception and nobody has any desire to make it otherwise. And I shall now repair thither for a Guinness, and I know perfectly well the song it will be—a glorious, full-bellied, heart-warming rendition of "John Peel." Good night.

♦ ♦ ♦

October 22, 1942, Eglinton, N. Ireland

I AM BACK in the 209th as executive officer of Battery I, a newly formed unit. I am second in command and find it interesting. We have a lot of instructing in the gentler arts of the Army and there are some new second Lieutenants who now look green to me, but I must have looked fully as foolish back in May. To think that I am an old experienced military man of one and a half years standing—five whole months as an officer and I should be calling anybody green!

We are at the base of one of Ireland's highest mountains and most beautiful views. The wind roars around us till our hut almost takes right off, and clouds that bump into the mountain top spill their rain on us at the most completely unexpected times. And a small river comes tumbling out of the woods right by us—a trip up along it is like a Wagnarian Rhine journey complete with all the bird songs and rocky cliffs and maybe even a fire at the top—I haven't traced it all the way yet. But it is a tremendous view and nothing can be as picture-like as the Irish Sea in a calm mood. It has an absolutely painted look about it.

Things are generally astir in the British Isles—people gathering in a record harvest, Yankees swamping the local populace, all sorts of mysterious whisperings going on, maybe somebody is doing something about everything finally.

❖ ❖ ❖

November

WE NOW HAVE the last chapter of the story that began back in the tepid 209th. I returned to a battery therein, performed ably, was in line for the job of battalion adjutant. Meanwhile a friend brought to my attention a certain bulletin requesting information as to officers who had traveled or spoke certain foreign languages. I traced the bulletin; took a nine-day leave in London, made certain contacts, went back to Ireland, and was suddenly thereafter transferred to the Signal Corps in the headquarters of the European Theatre of Operations. I can tell you absolutely nothing about my work, so be prepared for a series of letters discussing the fog, Bobbies and Sir Howard Button's family—anything but the Army, and that must be that. I am to go through some schooling, starting Monday, and with the start I already have, I should finally find myself in a war job that allows me to do something I can do.

It almost seems like a direct, foreordained path from the day when Fred Allen anointed me "The Mysterious Mr. Button." At least now I have a visible rank in the military hierarchy, but, alas, my work will have to remain as mysterious now as it was then.

5

London and Bletchley Park

LEAVING NORTHERN IRELAND was not easy. I had put down roots there. All I knew of my new duty was contained in the announcement that had appeared on the regimental bulletin board one day, requesting that any member of the command who possessed communications experience, a working knowledge of the German language, and the ability to resist the blandishments of glamorous foreign female spies should report forthwith to a certain address in London for assignment to a classified project. I had no idea what the activity was, but the requirements seemed in line with my qualifications. My NBC connection filled the first requirement and my *Wanderjahre* in Europe gave me the second. As to the third, I could hardly wait to put my patriotism to the test. I signed up, was immediately accepted and transferred to U.S. Army Signal Intelligence at Command Headquarters in London.

My arrival in London was eased by British hospitality that was short on rations, long on friendship. We helped with the rations and formed many valued friendships both in our work and social life in London. A hospitality center had been set up by the British in Grosvenor Square with a mission to invite lonesome Yanks into a British home for Christmas or other festive occasions (such as they could be). It was my encounter with this service that turned me around another corner in my life.

The hospitality desk was manned by an attractive British girl whose job, she said, was to match guest with host to the greatest degree of compatibility she could, given the wide divergence of accent and manners of the U.S. servicemen. But in my case this problem was quickly overcome. The girl asked me about my entertainment preferences; for example, did I like to have a date for dinner, or for a walk in the park, or to go to a movie, or did I want the "whole show"? I replied simply that I was deeply into music and liked the company of others who liked and understood music. Through her good offices I was presently invited to spend Christmas 1942 with a British family with three daughters and two pianos. Would that all of life's problems were so easily and so lavishly solved!

The family to which I was invited, or assigned, consisted of a widowed mother, a daughter who worked at the Bank of England, a second daughter who worked for the National Fire Service, and a third, the only unmarried one, who sang professionally on the stage. The songstress, Decima, sang grand opera, light opera, comic opera, and musical comedy and had been in recent productions of Leslie Henson, Bea Lillie, Noel Coward, Stanley Holloway, and other great names of the era. They had all lived through the worst of the Nazi blitz, and in the best tradition of the theater they kept the show going, and the people kept coming, bombs or no bombs. One had to admire them, and even love them, which I soon did, for their fortitude, their generosity, their historic legacy, and for the way one of them sang songs to which I played an accompaniment that seemed to catch her fancy.

At the Christmas party, Decima inevitably was asked to entertain the guests, which she agreed to do if perchance a pianist could be found among them. It was my big moment. I volunteered instantly, something one never does in the Army. In deference to the only American present, she chose a popular American song "You Made Me Love You" for her first number, one that I knew well. But she was only half way through it when the air raid siren entered into competition with her. I paused, wondering if we were supposed to obey the warning or the Muse. "Carry on," she said, "it's only the Germans," and carry on I did. The Muse won, she won, and I upheld the honor of the U.S. Army by finishing the song with her on a high note. I also won a future wife. It was later reported to me that on this occasion the family, having compared notes, concluded, "I was quite presentable, for an American." No obstacles were put in the way of our further meetings. As soon as ENSA (the British equivalent to our USO) found out that we were a viable international musical act, we were in demand at British military posts in the London area. For me, it was Army Signal Intelligence by day, and our own kind of vaudeville by night. We were a natural, compatible combination. Our musical styles were similar, our tastes the same. Our British audiences considered us examples of "lend-lease in reverse" and our programs were well received. The British thought they were getting the better part of the bargain, but I thought that I was.

Some two years later, when all troops designated for the Normandy invasion were quarantined along England's south coast, I among them, I managed to get a one-day pass to London. There I found a jeweler who had just the ring I had in mind. My soloist was then on tour in Nottingham. I could only ask the jeweler to mail it to her, which he did, but neglected to identify myself as the sender. The ring, an emerald and two diamonds, arrived in Nottingham on D-Day as I was preparing to embark for Normandy in two days. My erstwhile soloist, having no further evidence, nevertheless drew the correct conclusion about the meaning of this gift. (This I learned about a month later in a letter delivered to me in France.) Decima became my fiancée and later my wife. I became husband, eventually father and grandfather, but always her piano accompanist. The show still goes on.

✦   ✦   ✦

Once I arrived at the U.S. Signal Intelligence HQ in London, various minuets and parlor games were devised by the security people there before I gradually discovered the nature of my new assignment. It was what Secretary of War Henry L. Stimson described as "reading other peoples' mail," in this case, the codes and ciphers of the German Wehrmacht communications system. The Secretary at first deplored this practice as "unbecoming a gentleman." That is, until he discovered what a priceless asset it could be toward the security of the nation and the enhancement of his career.

Communications or signals intelligence might be regarded by some as an amoral game. Its practitioners around the world listen in to the messages of friend, foe, or potential foe alike. If their circumstances change, some willingly work for both sides. Thus many captured German signal intelligence personnel, who were graduates of U.S. or British universities, were quite willing to reverse their lingual skills to help us interpret their own signal traffic. Long before World War II, the U.S. services had been reading Japanese codes. But the British have had the longest involvement in the secret profession of signal or communications intelligence, with a record begun in the days of Queen Elizabeth I and her master spy and code-breaker Sir Francis Walsingham. To these two I pay obeisance. The Queen's intelligence system, compounded of ubiquitous spies and astute cryptographers, frustrated plans of the Pope, King Phillip of Spain, Mary Queen of Scots, and other pretenders, and through these means figuratively sank the Spanish Armada. By such skills, Great Britain emerged as the first truly world empire. I was about to be initiated into the incredible secret world created in the sixteenth century and now in full flower in the twenty-first century, enhanced by technology.

The Army provided me with an apartment, or flat, on Edgware Road, near Marble Arch. My ports of call, more or less daily, were the underground offices of the Army Signal Intelligence Service, the Officers Club on North Audley Street, and the Dorchester Hotel on Park Lane where tea was served at 4 PM. Hardly the trenches, one might say. At night the Luftwaffe paid frequent visits, which I could watch from the roof of my apartment building, but they did not seem to know their way around West London. It was noisy, people were getting killed daily, and piles of rubble grew and grew all over the city.

This had all been going on since 1940, of course, but then the British had no real ally. Many of our people in Congress were actively opposed to participation in Europe's periodic wars, and the British nation stood alone against their formidable foe. But by the time I arrived in London, it was clear that the U.S. decision to join Britain in her war against Hitler had been made, and it was only a matter of time before the Americans were to join wholeheartedly in the war against Nazi Germany.

In the fledgling U.S. Army Signal Intelligence Service, I was an uninitiated beginner in the bizarre and arcane business of intelligence. Everything was so secret it was hard to find out why I was there and what we were supposed to be doing. The British, of course, knew the game, as they had been playing it for three or four centuries. They were reluctant to let the Americans in on their secret, the hottest secret of WW II, for fear of a security breach. This secret was their success in breaking and reading the German Enigma code machine signals.

I was paired off with a British liaison officer assigned to us by the British to make sure, as I soon suspected, that the Americans did not find out too much, too soon, about what they were doing, and with what success. At that time the British were, in my opinion, the senior intelligence service, and they were not interested in relinquishing this position to the Americans as we began to create our own intelligence operation in London.

My British colleague was a delightful, sly, witty, intellectually astute Oxford graduate. As I was an English major in college, I found him the ideal companion for tours through English history, and in no time we had no secrets between us. At some point my British colleague began making vague and mysterious references to something called "BP." I had learned by this time that cryptanalysis had several levels of complexity, from low-grade three-letter codes up to machine-made ciphers of five-letter groups. All I ever saw around our London office were the low-grade codes, and soon I could solve some of these myself and even translate the German into readable English. But the intelligence thus gained was not going to win any wars. There had to be something else. I made cautious inquiries and soon learned that the "something else" was Bletchley Park (BP) and its success in penetrating German code transmitted through the Enigma machine. This was the method the Germans used for all their important military, naval, diplomatic, and police communications traffic. The British had solved the machine's operation, broken the code, and were daily reading its output at BP by intercepting enemy wireless communications through radio stations on a line from Wick, in northern Scotland, to the tip of Cornwall. This intelligence was being sent wherever it was needed, starting with the prime minister. So tight was security that the enemy, Germany, never caught on, and neither did the Americans, until the British gradually opened the BP door to their key ally.

The establishment at Bletchley Park, or "Station X" as it was called, wrought this miracle of code interception and decryption on a country estate in Buckinghamshire, bought by the government, some sixty miles north of London. This was the center of British code-breaking operations. Bursting with Nisson huts, it was populated by an assortment of college professors, technical wizards, military oddballs like myself, and eccentrics from every walk of life. Run by the military Government Code and Cypher School, there was absolutely no sign of military discipline. Admirals rode to work on bicycles. All ranks commingled for picnic lunches on the front lawn of the mansion. There were no prescribed uniforms—everyone wore what they looked good in. Social life was enhanced by the presence of lovely British women who worked at every task, menial and professional, and whose contribution to the mission was equal to that of the best there, regardless of rank.

Before any formal reciprocal agreements had been reached on complete intelligence sharing between the Americans and the British, I was admitted to Bletchley Park in the early spring of 1943, thanks to the trust of my British colleague and his confidence that the secret of their operation would never leak out through me. As one of the first Americans dispatched to BP, I had no instructions other than to find out what it was all about. I felt I had been assigned to somewhere in heaven in advance, perhaps, of being sent there by a hostile bullet. Once initiated into the "Ultra" society, and allowed to read the BP daily output, I could better understand why and how Great Britain had become the world power that it was, in spite of the power and might of its historic, and much larger, opponents.

Intelligence information resulting from intercepts and decryptions of enemy or neutral signal codes in the European Theater was given the code name "Ultra"; that produced at Arlington Hall, Virginia, was identified as "Magic" and was mostly concerned with the Pacific Theater. The British had broken the German code, while the Americans had penetrated the Japanese. Thus, while Hitler, Mussolini and Hirohito had their own Axis, we had one too, the Ultra-Magic Axis.

In the course of my indoctrination at BP, I was often told that had American signal intelligence been properly organized and processed, Pearl Harbor need not have happened at all. The British were not as deeply into Japanese codes as they were into the German, or if they were, they did not let on. The U.S. establishment on the BP level was at Arlington Hall, and it took a Pearl Harbor to animate and energize its contact with the British. This, too, has been adequately documented in the public media, with the possible exception of the case of Baron Oshima, Japanese ambassador to Berlin. The Baron was a frequent luncheon guest of Adolf Hitler. Their conversation covered all aspects of the war and of Hitler's diseased objectives and ambitions. The Baron reported all this to Tokyo in a Japanese code that was an open book at Arlington Hall. In fact, the Americans were reading the Baron's reports before they ever reached the Emperor, and the Baron went peacefully to his grave never suspecting that he had been a key player in the downfall of the entire Axis and the provider of the most interesting reading material in Washington. London and BP received all of this from Arlington Hall, and ultimately they reciprocated in kind, with all of the German Enigma intercepts after an unprecedented deal between two of the most secret intelligence agencies in the world, and our enemies never found out about it until the war was long over.

I quickly formed the view that I had found, in BP and all of its permutations, the key to understanding how history was made, how wars were started, won, or lost, how politicians' careers were made or broken, and international relations, both friendly and otherwise, were conducted even in peacetime. The technology of code-breaking at the highest level was of course beyond the comprehension of all but a select few. It was the interpretation of the information produced, and most important the use to which it was put by those allowed to see it, that provided me with a new career, a new worldview, and a feeling of kinship with all the historic figures, starting with Sir Frances Walsingham in the sixteenth century, who never spoke of their work but built their careers on it. The seventeenth-century *Camden Annals of British History* considered communications interceptions too private to be shared with the general public. And indeed they still are. These activities constitute the vital jugular vein of officialdom in England and every advanced nation in the world today. If this was to be my military specialty, it looked like far more fun than slamming shut the breechblock on a 155-millimeter cannon. And a lot safer.

There were four officers whose ambitions shaped my activities in London. Two of them were my superiors: Colonel Preston Corderman and Colonel George Bicher, at the Army Signal Corps. The third was my superior when I became a staff officer with G-2: Brigadier General Edwin Sibert, chief of intelligence on the staff of General Omar Bradley, Commander of 12th Army Group and the top American command in Europe. The fourth, Colonel Carter Clarke, was the newly appointed director of a mysterious entity in Washington, D.C., named the Special Branch, which had oversight of all U.S. code-breaking activities except those of the Navy. His direct access to the President indicated the importance of this group.

Some highly placed officers in the American Command thought they ought to have their own BP with an inter-service structure, but this was not, at that time, the American way of doing things. The Army had its routines, the Navy had its own. Each wanted to win the war in its own right. At Bletchley Park, the British had a sophisticated hybrid, with Army, Navy, RAF, and diplomats all sharing what they got from Ultra, the intercept product, and coordinating the overall response at the highest level.

Being one of the very first Americans to witness the full extent of the intelligence activities at BP, I was in a groundbreaking position as we set about re-creating BP with an American label. As a mere draftee, who by this time had reached only the rank of captain, I was actively involved in the formation of interservice sharing of intercept intelligence, which has grown into what is today the National Security Agency (NSA), with satellites and listening stations all over the world.

Up until the creation of Special Branch, the U.S. Army Signal Corps thought that signal intelligence, as well as management of our communications, was its prerogative. The General Staff intelligence component (G-2) considered the Signal Corps as just one of the many sources at its disposal, neither more nor less important than any other. Special Branch was the means by which Roosevelt's administration intended to resolve this intelligence turf war, and to coordinate American intelligence operations. It represented the American solution to everything: start up another department. As its chief, Colonel Clarke was in charge of the American relationship with BP, and was initially unaware of my assignment to BP (George Bicher having orchestrated it through a mid-level liaison officer). Much later he acknowledged my work with a personal note: "To Colonel Robert E. Button, whose penetrating intelligence and keen perception contributed materially to the success of many arcane projects during WW II" and signed Carter Weldon Clarke, Brigadier General.

It is strange to imagine, but I found myself squarely in the middle of two wars—one with the Germans and the other a turf war between G-2 and the Army Signal Corps, complicated by negotiations at the highest levels in London and Washington about sharing or not sharing what each side knew and did not really want to tell. A third war was going on between the U.S. Navy and everybody else, British as well as American, in the signal intelligence business, but this did not concern me. I was part of the Army but received such a thorough indoctrination into the British establishment that I could understand the British chagrin at seeing the Americans trying to duplicate all their work to produce an intelligence service based on a U.S. effort alone. It was all about control. As long as the British had a working Enigma system going, they maintained highest security and controlled what was given out and to whom it was given. This the Americans could not accept. Since I had developed a great affection and admiration for the British, turmoil in the intelligence world put me in a very difficult spot. Nothing in my military education had prepared me for such an experience. It was a mélange of history, politics, international relations in war and peace, high-level ambitions, and exposure to the technology that was giving birth to the modern computer age.

In my opinion, the person who made the most significant contribution to saving Great Britain and the winning of World War II, next to Sir Winston Churchill, was beyond doubt Alan Turing, about whom many people know nothing at all. Turing, a mathematician and author of a universal computing theory, was the father of today's computer. He conceived the methods and technology that in effect reversed the German cipher device known as the Enigma and made the German wireless traffic readable by the British. Turing's machines, known as "bombes" were able to unravel the wheel-settings for the Enigma ciphers thought by the Germans to be unbreakable. In fact, if one did not know the settings, the odds were a staggering 150 million to one against decryption. During the war, the cipher changed daily, but so efficient was Turing's machine that if Hitler sent orders to von Rundstedt, for example, Churchill would be reading the same orders in English before von Rundstedt had received them in German.

The German submarine fleet was sent to the bottom by the simple procedure of decoding their Enigma-coded reports, noting their positions, and directing the Navy to the location where countermeasures would be most effective. Turing's machine received and decoded the Luftwaffe's operations' orders for the attacks called the Battle of Britain, allowing the RAF to provide a most effective organized welcome whenever the Germans showed up to do battle. There were countless incidents of this nature, involving not only the military but also the diplomatic and espionage communities as well.

At BP, Turing was not especially admired for his lifestyle, but as a matter of fact, he was but one in a gaggle of eccentric geniuses whose personalities may have been odd but whose unerring talent for encryption analysis came up with the answers time and time again and assured Britain's survival. Nobody ever questioned whether Alan Turing was a dedicated patriot. Nobody cared particularly what his orientation was—that aspect of his private life which probably bothered him more than it did anyone else. He was quite simply a genius who found out how and where to serve his nation's war effort with his own talents and in his own style.

Initially, none of my superior officers in the Signal Corps, those to whom I supposedly reported, had any idea of the scope, range, or significance of what was being produced at Bletchley. The British fed our forces what they thought was good for us, mostly tactical military information, disguised as to its source. This was very useful in daily operations both in land battles and in the U-Boat war in the North Atlantic. During that period, nobody was allowed to reveal the role of communications interception, or signal intelligence, in the outcome of the war. Husbands could not speak of their war work to their own families. Because of the security blackout, those generals who rushed into print right after the war could make no mention of Ultra, but the generals' reputations could not stand the delay. As a result, one had to conclude that their military successes were due to sheer genius, what they learned at West Point or Sandhurst, or their own intuition. Yet none of these elements could have turned the tide of battle favorably to our cause without Ultra.

Since the Enigma-Ultra secret of Station X and its extraordinary importance to the war effort has now been revealed to the public through books, memoirs, movies, and television, I will not fully detail the stories. Suffice it to say, many consider the activity at Bletchley

Park to have shortened the war by at least two years. Its first major success was to give the British knowledge of Germany's plans to invade their country in 1940. They forthwith launched bombing attacks on all the French channel ports, destroying the barges that lay ready to transport German soldiers, and the German airfields in occupied France.

The following year, by solving the German U-Boat Atlantic Enigma key, the British gathered information that enabled them to break the stronghold that the U-Boat packs had on Britain's only lifeline—the Atlantic convoy ships from Halifax to England. Sir Harry Hinsley, a good friend of mine and now deceased, headed the British Navy's code-breaking intelligence operation at BP, intercepting all German naval wireless traffic. Once the German code was broken, the British were able to target and sink the German submarine supply ships stationed mainly off Brazil. They also were able to target submarines headed back to the port of Wilhelmshaven, Germany, based on intercepted positioning reports. These efforts came none too soon, as Britain was on the verge of being starved out within six weeks. Another success from wireless intercepts was the interruption of German supplies being sent from Italy to North Africa. Ultra revealed the names of the ships, the timing of their departure, and the timing of their arrival in North Africa, whereby the British Navy was able to cut off the traffic and starve Rommel out of the African war.

As is well known, the communications intercepts and deciphering that went on at Bletchley Park helped make possible the success of our invasion on the Normandy beaches. As the date for this event approached, camps were established on the south coast of England for all participants. As a liaison intelligence officer on General Bradley's staff, I was assigned to the Intelligence Office of the British Headquarters in one of these camps near Southampton, where we received a constant flow of information derived from intercepts of the German Army units in France. These communications intercepts and the French resistance (or Maquis) were our two best sources of intelligence. While high-level codes were broken at Bletchley Park, we also received a wealth of lower-level intercepts and decoding that came to us direct from the British and American intercept detachments in the field. Our goal was to evaluate this enormous flow of data and determine what opposition we would be facing in France. Synthesizing and analyzing intelligence continued to be my job after I crossed over to France with the British Army and ultimately rejoined Bradley's 12th Army Group moving through France and into Luxembourg.

6

Letters from London

ONCE I BEGAN working in intelligence, my duties and military activities were top secret and could not be written or spoken about. Luckily, however, there was sufficient material for my letters home based on a social life that blossomed from contacts made at the U.S. Officers Club on Audley Street, through British officers who came to our office and at the Royal Air Force Signal Camp where I was sent to practice wireless and intercepts. Many English women were in uniform and in the war thought it their duty to accommodate the Americans who had come to help them win the war. They may have been following orders from the top—word had come down from Churchill to "be nice to the Americans"—or it may have been that a single male in his twenties who could play the piano was considered an asset at any party. In any event, British hospitality seemed to me to be most genuine and extraordinarily generous.

From a continuous stream of invitations I had much to write about, and write I did—about a sherry party thrown by Mrs. Anthony Eden, tea dances at Grosvenor House, a particularly memorable dinner dance at the Savoy, New Year's Eve at Bill Astor's (son of Lady Astor), tea with the granddaughter of Charles Dickens, Easter service at a thousand-year-old church, and Christmas with my future wife, Decima, and her family. Then, too, I could write about the atmosphere of London during the bombings and the daily pleasures of taking tea whether it was at a grand manor house or in my tent while waiting with the British Army to cross the Channel.

Expounding upon my off-duty life may appear to some as frivolous in a time of war, but I like to believe it gave my parents a sense of comfort and knowledge about their soldier boy. Their knowledge of war was drawn only from accounts of life in the trenches of World War I and I sought to reassure them by writing about everything but life in the trenches, or death in the various forms I observed, or hand-to-hand combat in which I never took part anyway. I'm sure they knew I could not have been promoted from a first lieutenant to a captain in eighteen months' time simply by performing a fine foxtrot or playing a mean piano.

Since my letters were written out of love and concern for my parents, my hatred of war and all its ugliness does not appear in them except by inference. In addition, I like to think the tone and content may have lightened the load of the censors.

❖   ❖   ❖

14 December 1942, U.S. Army Signal Section, Force HQ, London

YESTERDAY BEING SUNDAY, I undertook to do what most officers do on Sunday afternoons, namely attend the tea dance at Grosvenor House, presided over by Lady Townsend and a host of lesser Ladies, each of whom acts as hostess at a table, with the assistance of the prettiest young damsels she can collect (from the ranks of the most socially acceptable, of course). One enters the ballroom and if it is the first time, one is shown to a table and there the Hostess introduces one around the circle. Then one dances and has tea, this process consuming the hours of 4 PM to 7PM. At one point in the afternoon there is a pause while a British and an American (or other Allied officer) together light a candle signifying friendship and brotherhood. I happened, the first time, to go to the table of Mrs. Coleridge-Davis, whose daughter Rosemary looked so much like cousin Ann Denny Easton that I called her Ann Denny instead of Rosemary, which amused her no end. But this wasn't all. It developed that the woman assisting Mrs. Coleridge-Davis was a Mrs. Conyers-Baker, and when I explained that Conyers was one of our names, we all turned into one happy family. Rosemary sings; so does her Ma, and in fact the latter had a musical career until she took time out to have three kids. Now she is going back to singing. Thursday I am going to dinner there and it will no doubt be a very musical evening with Mrs. D. singing long-hair and Rosie a slightly more bar-room than salon variety. All of this is usually accompanied by a couple of air raids.

I have not announced to Sir Howard Button that I've returned; this because I wanted to see how much time off my job would leave me before committing myself to a string of social amenities. He has in mind luncheon at Parliament, dinner at the London County Council, and such affairs. I must go pretty slow on my outside activity, because there's such a great deal to absorb in actual work. If there was ever a moment when first things must come first, this is it.

That doesn't mean, however, that I could afford to miss the Tchaikovsky Concerto that the London Symphony played Saturday afternoon, as per the enclosed program. The soloist was about my age and very sure of every note. The Fourth Symphony I think has very little in it; it is a half hour of strident melancholy and not even profoundly sad. But the Concerto was worth sitting thru the other two. And as usual, I came away wondering why the British have the reputation of being unmusical. Perhaps they don't compose prolifically, but they stand in line all day for seats, and respond most vociferously when they like or dislike something, and they always know exactly what they think when they do.

English families have sent in requests for U.S. officers as Christmas guests—by the hundreds. I and two colleagues have accepted a delightfully worded invitation from a family who have a piano, like music both high-brow and low, and who spend Xmas eating, drinking, playing games or dozing by the fire, just as one pleases. We take things with us, like some sugar, butter, bacon, cigarettes, etc.—things that we can get at the P.X. and the British are currently doing without. It sounds like fun. These people are the most hospitable in the world. The only thing that hurts them is the way some Americans throw their money around—our pay is fantastic compared to what they get.

The post office is by now so confused over my change of address that I don't expect the mail to catch up for months. It's probably all over in Ireland. I haven't received any since I left there, but I know why, so I am not grousing over it.

❖   ❖   ❖

29 December 1942

I HAD A marvelous Xmas at the home of the Knight family. We arrived at 12:30 laden with our parcels and the size and variety completely astounded our hosts. Mrs. Knight, a widow, was a wonderful cook. Decima, the youngest daughter, was the musical one. Margaret Knight Lait was next; her husband was either captured or killed at Singapore and nothing has ever been heard of him. Phyllis, the eldest, had a husband in India, and there was a brother, Bill, with the 8th Army in Egypt.

We started with a round of drinks. It took Decima and me about two minutes to get into music, and we never stopped all day after that except to eat. She is most attractive, a beautiful singer of both long-haired and swing music. In the show she did some Russian things with dancing, and some waltz songs.

Dinner commenced at 2:30 and lasted a good two hours, when it was closely followed by a lavish tea. One never stopped eating and drinking at all. There were two pianos in the rather large living room, and every piece of music you could think of.

Mrs. Knight and her three daughters went all thru the blitz, and from what I have seen of small air raids, that must have been a severe trial for four females by themselves. They seem to have lost nothing by it but a few panes of glass from nearby bombs, and they must have gained much confidence. They typify what people mean by the British being able to "take it," for in spite of the war having come so close to them, they are as cheerful and merry a bunch as you'd ever find.

Decima is full of fun and not at all "touched" by stage work. She is a girl of much character, absolutely indomitable spirit and a perfectly true ear. She was educated in a Church of England convent and was most properly brought up. She has made her own living since she was fifteen (is now twenty-three), and is somewhat better than I am at tennis.

❖ ❖ ❖

8 January 1943

LONDON IS VERY much like New Jersey as far as climate is concerned. The same overcast sky, or sometimes a clear brisk morning with powdery snow in the gutters, the same look about things as people hurry home from work at 5:30, just barely beating the Blackout. Usually at about 5:30 I leave the office and go either to the Officers Club or the American Nurses Club—both places are equally good for dining and there's always somebody to dine with at each place. After dinner I either study some language or visit somebody who happens to have a piano. I've met some very interesting families, one a sculptor and one a painter—the latter in a huge old house with complete pine walls so that the whole thing smells either like a woods or a clothes chest. The ceiling is two stories up and portraits of everyone from Churchill down to mere Indian princes stand around the room. A large Bechstein piano stands there and it sounds wonderful in such a tremendous room. The family being Irish, we get along very well.

❖   ❖   ❖

13 January 1943

YESTERDAY MRS. ANTHONY Eden, wife of the Foreign Secretary, threw a sherry party to which I was invited along with various other staff members, Balkan diplomats, diplomat's ex-wives, generals of every Allied Nation there is, and finally Anthony himself. I had a good half hour with him on the general topics of Anglo-American relations and various measures which might be taken to improve his wife's musical taste. She likes it "low and hot" she said, which her husband deplored. I met Jan Masaryk, Lady Mountbatten, Clive Brook and his wife, the former Premier of Yugoslavia, a Greek general, a Serbian general, a Czech general, an American general, Lord Milne, Lady Leigh, etc., etc. and had my picture taken in the same group with Mr. Eden and his wife and the Yank general—this at Mr. Eden's insistence, which was nice of him, I thought.

Mr. Eden was more pleased than anything at the comment that we (our generation) choose more and more to disregard differences in British and U.S. nationality and it was this that led to our further conversation. He was perfectly informal and very easy to talk with. He said that we should meet again—a matter that Mrs. E. would arrange—and what pleased me—offered a few compliments on a couple of positions I took on different matters. After the war he is going to Florida and lie on a beach for four years without moving, he said. We discussed his stand of 1930–31 when he tried to make noise about Germany and didn't dare become too obstreperous about it. He said that if he had known then what he learned later, he wouldn't have hesitated to make a complete nuisance of himself in a drastic attempt to best some of his then superiors. But then he wouldn't have become Foreign Secretary, probably, or at least not so soon. There was an interesting moment as he, the perfect Englishman, sought to evade an old dowager called Lady Walker; she was trying to say goodnight, but would have been verbose and fatuous even if she hadn't been slightly sozzled, and poor Eden was almost desperate. He applied the polite brush-off, the apologetic retreat, and finally the strategic withdrawal, which left the old busybody nothing to do but say goodnight to which he replied over his shoulder. Lady W. married millions—which she kept telling people—and is also a Yank, but after hearing her I felt ashamed to admit her as a compatriot.

Tonight I am having dinner with a Welsh artist, his Russian wife, daughter, another British couple (he in the intelligence service) and a Navy "Leftenant." One never knows what nationality will turn up. There is quite a contest going on to see who can date up the three beautiful daughters of King Zog who lives nearby. Speaking of mix-ups, his wife is a Hungarian Catholic, he is the Mohammedan king of Albania, his mother was American and goodness knows what else he has hidden away. But his daughters, being "Princesses," are too grand to go dashing around like ordinary folk. Or maybe they daren't face the ordinary competition.

I am playing for some more RAF and Red Cross events on Sundays and getting into some terrific gatherings in the process. The RAF can throw a beautiful party and they certainly must have all the whiskey in the British Isles. But they certainly hold it well. My observation leads me to the conclusion that Yanks are better company sober; British better tight.

✦ ✦ ✦

20 January 1943

LAST SUNDAY I joined our troops for a concert at a British establishment on the outskirts of London. As is the usual procedure, we met at the theater where the others are playing in London's best current revue, and the British Army had six Daimlers there to take us. The group consists generally of Leslie Henson; probably the best known British funnyman, Douglas Byng; another headline comedian, Dorothy

Dickson; a real old-timer and a group of six chorus girls; a couple of actors and actresses for parts in sketches; Decima Knight, who sings both long-haired and Yankee short-haired music; and I, who now both accompany Decima and play a solo or two which goes over beautifully no matter how many keys on the piano don't work—my uniform helps out when I miss notes. That is the show, and it runs a good two hours without dragging. The humor is very broad, to put it politely, and the forces love it. The gang are wonderful both on and off the stage and they have accepted me as something of a novelty I think—an American who can do something with a slightly cultural twist and to emphasize this I chew gum and use corny slang as a contrast.

Well, we left at about 5 PM and headed for the suburbs. It was an ordnance depot we were looking for, but every time the driver stopped to ask directions of a civilian, the latter would say, "Audience depot? What on earth is that?"—until we began to wonder how we could use the term "audience depot" and have it mean something. Henson finally hit upon it as we were passing a graveyard!

We put on a show that progressed very well for half an hour until suddenly, as Byng was cracking some of his broadest jokes, the air raid sirens went off, rising and falling in close thirds that every now and then all arranged themselves to form an almost supernatural chord. There is nothing scary about the sirens—just sort of sad. Hardly anybody in the audience heard them, but everyone who was an Air Raid Warden had to leave for a post, and poor Doug thought they were just persons leaving because they were shocked at his jokes. I had done my playing (Rhapsody in Blue) and went outside to watch the fireworks. The sirens only go off when raiders are in the immediate vicinity. They were, soon enough. Guns a long way off began to hammer, and position after position took up the fire as they came nearer. Finally the guns right in the next fields took off, and we could hear planes right overhead. I reflected that there might be better places to spend a raid then in an ordnance depot, but the Germans paid no attention to us or our show, and went on to bomb elsewhere. We could see gun bursts all around the sky, and the rumble of AA guns was continuous, like thunder, on all sides.

It stopped in about an hour, and the show was still going its way, nobody in the audience having stirred out of their seats. In the dressing room there was such a chatter of talk you couldn't even hear the AA guns. And just as if it were part of the Air Raid Precaution system, at the first siren the door opened and in popped a flunkey with two more bottles of gin!

After the concert there was a gay party at the Officers' Mess, and we finally took off for town at about 11:30. I have a more or less standing invitation.

At about 4:30 AM the sirens started up again and this time it was slightly different. You can't be so objective about it when you're in bed. The distant guns began, and gradually the nearer ones, till bang off went the local battery and I nearly popped out of bed. Then a short bit of silence, in the middle of which a swoosh and a rumble that shook the entire house. At this I thought I'd better have a look around. Mrs. Knight was in the kitchen making tea, but nobody else was up, and so I took up a post by the window to watch the gun bursts all around the sky. Nothing else landed near us but the anti-aircraft artillery guns banged away for an hour and then everything quieted down. I went back to bed. At breakfast the three Knight sisters took the position that it was only a baby raid of no importance—"You should have seen the Blitz"—but I thought it was a very brisk show for my first, and I'd just as soon enter the thing gradually.

Of course everyone expected the raid to be repeated the next night and the subway stations were full of sleepers, wardens, mobile hot-food posts and everything in well-organized preparation for a blitz. However there was only a short alert and nothing happened. But we carry our helmets around now, just in case.

Today at noon they pulled a surprise raid coming in low, and I could see the gun bursts down the road from my apartment building. The public is very raid-wise and the services are so well organized that the minute an alert sounds, everything falls into its proper place and people seem to know exactly what to do. They crowd into the subway stations with bedding and food.

Although recent raids are nowhere near blitz proportions, the AA defense is said to be in greater volume than London ever had before. There is some satisfaction in this even if there are bound to be some bombs dropped in every raid, anti-aircraft or not.

❖   ❖   ❖

Spring, 1943

THIS IS THE first letter in about two weeks as I have been off in the country at a British establishment learning some secret things. I must say, they are a pleasant people to work with. Amongst themselves, even unpleasant things are handled nicely, politely, and gracefully; as far as making a Yankee feel at home and well-looked-after, they simply can't be beaten. One works away and suddenly a cute little A.T.S. [British women's army] corporal appears with a cup of morning coffee and a piece of cake; one works a bit more and up comes one's colleague with a handful of pears and apples sent up by his wife (whom one hasn't even met). Afternoon has hardly had time to get tiresome by tea-time (also with cake), and dinner is regularly preceded by several beers around which nobody talks shop.

I was billeted in a pub called "The Bull." This was in a town called Stony Stratford, on the Watling road between London and Birmingham, the oldest road in the British Isles, supposedly. Three doors from The Bull was "The Cock." In the old coaching days coaches from London stopped at the Bull, while the ones from Birmingham stopped at the Cock, and the drivers told their respective stories in their respective Inns. By the time the Birmingham story had been retold in the London crowd and vice versa, you can see why the natives developed the idea of a "cock and bull" story, and this is supposed to be the very origin of the phrase.

I was up and out for many a meadow stroll before breakfast out there. It was delightful country. In the fields early you could hear all the waking-up sounds—dogs, cattle bells, trains in the distance, children, village bells—and see a clear sky just beginning to warm up with the morning sun. The only really modern sound would be a fleet of bombers starting out for somewhere in the direction of Berlin.

❖   ❖   ❖

16 June 1943, England

NOT ONLY DO I fail to perceive any possibility of flying home for a weekend leave, but I have the distinct impression that it will be a fairly long while before I get back on any basis. This fact is something for an American to face; but to a British family it would be nothing at all out of the ordinary. For centuries they have been scattering their families all around the world and they think it quaint that one should even pause at the thought of three or four years abroad.

Being a captain makes some difference in my pay but not in my work. I get $200 a month plus living allowances now. That is, I will, starting with June 30th paycheck. One is entitled to be a captain at any age, practically, above about twenty-five or twenty-six; hence I have it fairly young and sooner, I think, than if I had stayed in the anti-aircraft business. The only time I feel a slight nostalgia for the AA is when the Germans come over, which they do every night after the moon gets beyond the crescent stage. You will think I'm getting blasé, but I can actually sleep thru guns, sirens and planes sometimes now and not know there has been a raid until the radio announces it next morning. The raids aren't heavy, but the guns make a terrific uproar, and, I might add, a very satisfying one.

❖   ❖   ❖

20 August 1943, Signal Section Force HQ

THE PHONE RANG and it happened to be a Mrs. Goode, whose daughter must have just become twenty-two or twenty-three or some nice eligible age; would I join a dinner party at the Savoy 7:45 Thursday evening? I struggled to recall where I had met the daughter, but concealed my confusion long enough to accept. When I met them the next night at the Savoy I finally remembered the daughter and everything proceeded smoothly under the lubricating effect of gin and Dubonnet. At such gatherings there is always a fabulously rich and sportive aunt to set the party off on a sound fiscal note. The aunt in this case was a Mrs. Pete Bennett, a well-known and most cosmopolitan Norwegian lady awash with diamonds, pearls and natural gifts of equal value. There was the usual eligible Naval lieutenant, the equally eligible and fashionably be-moustached British Army Captain, a beautiful young Army wife whose husband was in India, the daughter, Valerie, a typically reticent, proper and dignified damsel whose instincts one assumed to have been trained in the Victorian school, and the uncle, also Norwegian, somewhat tolerant of the young people but quite ready to discuss the affairs of Lever Bros. or Barclay's Bank. Such was the party. We had a lobster soufflé, red wine, then roast chicken and fresh peas, and a fruit cup with peaches, custard and rum flavor. Then dancing and several pitchers of lager. The daughter danced heavily and talked; the young wife, who was Irish, out-sparkled everyone but the Norwegian aunt, who, tho a grandmother, had an amazing store of vitality—maybe she absorbed some from the diamonds. She didn't drink or smoke, and she looked about forty. But in spite of these two attractions one strove to make the proper fuss over the daughter and not to have too good a time dancing with the others, who, of course, were merely to provide sort of a backdrop for the activity around the daughter. This merry scene went on till 11:45 when somehow the Norwegian uncle produced a taxi and we all went home. It was a delightful evening and just the sort of thing one needs periodically. The Savoy is the best place in London for an evening's dinner dancing, in spite of the nightly German air raids.

❖ ❖ ❖

13 October 1943

We had quite a visit from the Germans last week. As usual the guns made more rumpus than the bombs, but a very comforting noise it was and you think all the while, "the more the better." Londoners no longer dash to shelters, but instead wait until nearby AA guns start. Only then does it seem that it's about time to go below. Before then it's like a Maplewood Fourth of July evening, with everyone standing around saying ooh and aah. It's hard to believe the Germans haven't got some trick up their sleeves besides a mere old-fashioned night airraid, but it is also hard to imagine a trick of war for which the British would not have a satisfactory counter-measure, so one doesn't worry at all. This is an unbeatable team, in spite of what some of our dimwitted Senators say. The tour those Senators made over here was a matter of finding soldiers from their home states and asking the boys to tell the home folks how the Senators had been seen over here "getting the real dope." Well, their uninformed, unintelligent, unconsidered statements in Washington cause us only embarrassment, and one doesn't hesitate to admit it. Roosevelt gained stature here, if possible, by the way he told them off.

❖ ❖ ❖

October 23, 1943

Every night for the past seven or eight the wretched miserable Germans wake us up with their one or two efforts.

I say—you should see London fire engines. They have no sooner begun than they leave off. That is to say, they are short. But their ladders go up just as high as any U.S. hook and ladder company does. Where, then, does the ladder go when it comes down? Who can say. The answer does not appear to the naked eye, although any fireman will tell you that the naked answer does on occasion appear to the eye. First you see miles of ladder extending up into ye olde stratosphere, one fireman on the top, spraying passing bombers, or firing machine guns at the Luftwaffe, and then at the sound of a gong the whole array compresses itself into a two-by-four truck that you could drive around our dining-room table without even asking Dad to move his chair in so you could get past the sideboard. Actually there are so many alleys and olde worlde lanes in this town that the fire engines have to be able to go in and out of everything but manholes. They are marvelous machines—solid, heavy, noisy, powerful and compact—complete with every possible gadget including tea service and all on a wheel base about equal to my old Ford. And it would take a tank to stop them.

◆ ◆ ◆

October 1943

THE OTHER DAY I suddenly found myself with five days leave and a standing invitation from the Oswald Birleys on my hands. (Birley is the portrait painter who has done the King, Queen, Prime Minister and other dignitaries.) So, I leaped aboard my bicycle, took enough extra rations of sugar etc. to prevent my becoming a nuisance and headed South. It was a glorious, warm autumn day with a clear sky and I was on the road by 8 AM. Route—Red Hill, Reigate, Haywards Heath, Lewes, New Haven, Seaford, Alfriston and Charleston Manor, the Birleys' country estate. When I arrived the good Scottish cook had huge dishes of baked fish and cheesed potatoes and beans, with hot apple pie for dessert all of which I had plenty of use for, as it took me all day to get to the coast from London. Cycling is the only way to get to know a country. You catch every detail of the landscape, and the places you pick for a pause and some coffee are more than likely ones that in a car you'd whiz right by. The country south of London is much like N.J.—rolling hills, none very high, farms, patches of woods, but the view usually has more in it, more well-arranged valleys with the church steeple exactly where it should be in a clump of trees by a stream, and the pub at just the right central corner of the village. There are attempts at modern housing here and there but they don't look at all permanent, whereas the old thatched-roof dwellings besides looking more comfortable seem to have always been there and to have no intention of ever not being there.

The Birleys' household is very well appointed. First a chambermaid tells you where everything is, and then whisks away your belongings into their proper corners. Suddenly tea and biscuits and jam happens; this you take in the "long" room, or living room, which has all the heavy beam work, period furniture, huge fireplace and deep easy chairs in front. Also, a Steinway grand, which I did not neglect. I settled down with a book (by W. Churchill) between tea and dinner; about two hours after dinner I was in bed. The bedroom was completely modern, with Olde Englishe leaded glass windows, pale blue sheets and a fat puff which was welcome. Nothing happened then till the maid brought tea at 8:30 AM and thereafter followed a wonderful farm breakfast of eggs and all the fixings.

Mr. Birley was going shooting so I went along. We managed fourteen rabbits of a particularly good eating variety. This was with the help of nets, two ferrets and a boy to manage them. The ferrets chase the rabbits out of the burrow either into a net or into the field; if the latter, we popped at them with shotguns now and then bagging one.

Lunch was as welcome as you can imagine after a morning in the open and afterwards I spent the afternoon riding my bike around thru the ancient villages in the vicinity. They are all the sites of castles of King Alfred, King Aethelred, King Harold, King Arthur and all the early Britons; in some cases even the flint walls remain. Everything in

Sussex is built out of flint because it's right underfoot and incidentally makes an attractive type of building.

The next few days passed in equally idle and pleasant circumstances, I making a real effort to finish Churchill (about nine hundred pages) and taking walks with Mrs. B. or cycling or mowing part of the lawn. Mr. B. was an Intelligence captain in the last war and knows (and has painted) practically everyone. He even speaks of Churchill as "Winston." At the moment he is painting the portrait of the new Chancellor of ye olde Exchequer, which ought to be a profitable undertaking.

Come Sunday, I didn't feel I could cycle back to London so I took the train.

This leave was a necessary interval betwixt two jobs. I have graduated from a special section to the main staff as the representative of that section. My address therefore is no longer "Signal Section—Force HQ," but instead, just "Force HQ" alone. This is the best possible break especially at this time. It doesn't mean I am a major yet, because one has to be Capt. for at least six months to be even eligible.

Mom, such has been the kindness and hospitality of Mr. and Mrs. Birley that it wouldn't be at all amiss for you to drop her a note or a gift.

◆ ◆ ◆

2 November 1943

MESSRS. ROYAL and Trammell (V.P. and President of NBC) came to London, parked at Claridges' and studied various aspects of the war for a couple of weeks. My good friend Howard Mussbaum, formerly of NBC and in fact the one who produced the "Crazy Heart Blues," is a public relations major here, threw a cocktail party for the two visitors. I had a good chat with each and also with Irving Berlin, who turned up. Mr. Trammell told me that if the Wall Street bid for the Blue Network had been the same amount as the other bid, he still would not have sold it to the Wall Street syndicate because he would have been accused by some people as selling out to the plutocrats, and giving the banks an element of control over broadcasting. Not that he was opposed to this in principle, but by selling to somebody else he could avoid that type of criticism. As a matter of fact, out of the $8,000,000 purchase price, $4,000,000 was cash and the rest a line of credit with several banks.

As for Irving Berlin—when the party reached the musical stage I could think of plenty of tunes by Jerome Kern, Oscar Hammerstein et al. but only two of Berlin's—"Always" and "Blue Skies." So I played those over a few times. Irving refused to sing a solo, but I'm told it's better if he doesn't sing at all.

I had tea with Charles Dickens's granddaughter last Sunday afternoon. She lives across the street from here. A nice friendly woman, who likes bridge and has been bombed out of her original home. Her name is Mrs. Elaine Waley.

❖ ❖ ❖

8 November 1943

LAST NIGHT'S BOMB was the closest I have been to yet. We have a mournful Minnie serenading us every night. Last night I was out at Decima's house sitting in front of the fire eating cake and drinking tea between sessions of practicing on arias from "Tosca." We heard the plane make a dive, come closer to the neighborhood and then a small earthquake when the bomb hit not so far away. Other than in cases like this, nobody pays the slightest attention to raids and often as not unless they happen to be in one's particular borough, one doesn't hear them at all.

❖   ❖   ❖

19 December 1943

LAST WEEK I played accompaniments at two concerts with Decima Knight. One was at a ball for the ARP of Hendon, a suburb; and the other was a dance in Holborn. She makes a tremendous hit and is best on the light classics, altho we do an occasional jazz number and quite often take olde English folk-songs from Shakespeare's times and make them into modern arrangements. This always goes down quite well, she being English and the inference to the audience being that the slightly disrespectful treatment of the piece is due to the Yank accompanist.

❖   ❖   ❖

20 December 1943

I WROTE JAN about an evening I spent in the English Speaking Union, and you have probably heard about that by now. Well, there was a Mrs. Guinness there, Gloria Ashford Guinness, formerly of Washington, who invited me to a charity function at the Mayfair where in turn I met an RAF pilot who invited me to go up on his night-fighter patrol (being as I am a qualified machine-gunner); also some other nice people of the Anglo-American set; and I was invited to a debutante party (last night) for Lady Dicks-Meades' daughter who has just come twenty-one.

So let's begin from there. I went to their home, a very large place with full suits of armor standing around on pedestals. Her husband, Sir Charles, is a famous sculptor, and had just finished a bust of Churchill himself. They had an orchestra and a bevy of lovelies, one of whom turned out to be a very talented singer. In no time at all we arranged a program, and to everyone's complete astonishment, and I might modestly add delight, we had a joint Anglo-American piano-voice recital that scored a complete success. British people are so happy when they find an American who can actually do something artistic or educated. I have never been so spoiled by applause in my life; altho my technique is not improving, the relative value of my playing is. Americans I'm afraid have too much of a hell-raising and gum-chewing reputation here, which persists in spite of the fact that the British can forgive almost anything in their desire to be friendly and to make us enjoy their country. I went to Mrs. Coleridge-Davis' home for dinner and played there too, and one of the ladies there immediately announced that apparently I had been either a pupil of Leschetizky's or had been taught by a pupil of his. At each such affair there will be half a dozen ladies or families with large Bechstein grands at home which want playing on, so you can see that I no longer lack either pianos or good families whose company I can enjoy any time.

I am living in a West End flat with an Air Force Major and another Lt. as roommates. We have a maid who gets breakfast for us; I get up at 7 AM, eat and get to the office at 8:30. I work till 5:30, study certain languages and other stuff at night and get to bed by 11. It's dark when I get up, and dark when I leave the office, so that I begin to feel something like a mole. But such continual blackout living makes the lighted interiors that much more cheerful. We have had no air raids or even warnings lately and one doesn't talk about the past ones any more than he can help. Besides, there are too many bomb holes around to let you forget what happened once.

✦   ✦   ✦

27 December 1943, G-2 Force HQ

XMAS EVE THERE occurred a party in a rather hard-to-find place; hence the host had prepared certain maps showing how a reasonably intelligent person might, from a given spot (Knightsbridge station), find his way thru the blackout to the destination. On the map were indicated stops where the thirsty might refresh themselves en route—this type of thing being known as a pub crawl. Decima Knight accompanied me on this quaint junket; we set forth at 6:30 PM and immediately found our first stop, the Bedford Arms. Two stiff drinks, please. Thence we followed the map to the next stop, the Dukes Head; two more, to help dispel the darkness. Next the Goat and Compasses (which comes originally from "God Encompasseth Us"), by which time it didn't seem dark at all. Eventually we reached our hosts' abode where there were lots of officers with their madams, all pleasantly fried and of nicely conglomerated nationalities (the madams). This function was pleasantly punctuated with bursts of song, some ribald, some seasonal, some religious but all lusty, and thus we wiled away many pleasant hours and brought out many memories. At about 10:30 PM the party broke up, nobody wanting to miss the last conveyances homeward; I must say that there is much virtue and sense in beginning parties at 6 and ending at 10; you have had enough of everybody by then anyhow, and you get enough sleep to have another real soon.

Apparently not having worn out my welcome at the Knights, I was invited there again for Xmas day. It hardly seemed that a whole year had passed, and that at the same hour, 11:30 AM, I was on the same bus, no. 73, going to the same place in 1943 as I was in 1942. The Knight females were in the same state of undress when I arrived and there was the same dash to cover. I was planted before the fire, given a bottle of soda and one of scotch, and left to my own thoughts while everyone else got dressed. Mrs. Knight was working on a turkey of about fifteen or eighteen pounds, and taking small sips of orange squash as she worked. Finally people foregathered for the opening of presents, or as Decima calls them, "presidents." They all gave each other clothing items and things they had made themselves; it is marvelous to behold what resourceful people can do with practically nothing to start from. I gave Mrs. Knight two packs of American playing cards with gilt edges, a thing the English haven't been able to buy for years. These and the other "presidents" I got at our P.X. Also I gave Mrs. K. a

Turkish towel, a washcloth and a face towel. Washcloths are very rare and on coupons, if you do get them, and poor quality at that. But ours are U.S. manufacture and very good. To Margaret, Sister #1, I gave a washcloth and face towel. To Phyllis, Sister #2, a bottle of Hinds Honey and Almond cream. To Decima, #3, the one box of candy we have been allowed to buy, a Whitman's Sampler, completely pre-war. Poor Decima could only squeak—the sight of such a box left her completely speechless. They wanted to take pictures of it rather than eat it. I was glad that it pleased them so much, because the turkey dinner was every bit as welcome to me. Mrs. Knight is adept at making food attractive. We ate steadily for an hour or so; turkey, string beans, peas, stuffing, bacon, sausage, potato, pudding, brandy sauce, canned peaches, chocolate sponge, mince pie, coffee and nuts. And port. This is not by way of saying that the Knights are wealthy and deal on the black market. Far from it. They just save all year for the Christmas feast and when the day arrives, they withhold absolutely nothing. For instance, the pudding, with raisins and brandy sauce. Raisins are on points, and I know she had been putting away a stock of raisins ever since July; the sauce was made with at least two or three weeks solid butter ration, but she had saved that too, and there it was, rich and sweet and full of kick as any sauce you ever tasted. The peaches I brought from the P.X., also a large tin of tomato juice, which also delighted them as it is practically unknown to the civilians.

At about 6:00 PM, Decima and I went to a party at the home of one of our lieutenants from West Orange who has married a wee Scot lassie here. We sang Christmas carols and hymns, of which "Good King Wenceslas" and "God Rest Ye Merrie Gentleman" seemed most fitting in dark, foggy London, with their combination of majors and minors somehow expressing the gloom outside and the cheer within. This went on till ten; then to bed, as Sunday the 26th is an ordinary working day, altho I, in the office at this moment, appear to be doing no work.

We expect that the appointment of Eisenhower as Supreme Allied Commander will untie a great many baffling knots that had arisen here because of the absence of a supreme boss to tell everyone what to do. It also should mean that we get down to brass tacks in short order and cut out a great deal of the wasteful effort that comes of having two supreme commands, ours and the British, existing side by side yet not combined in an operating sense. This appointment should clear the atmosphere a great deal. I wouldn't say that it should have been Marshall because I think he is probably the only stable individual in the whole U.S. war effort and the most valuable, the President included; hence he should be where he is, because if the invasion gets difficult, blame will always descend on the general leading it, who can be displaced if necessary, but I don't know where could be found another person who could administer things as well as Marshall, regardless of the successes or reverses in particular operations.

✦ ✦ ✦

2 January 1944

NEW YEAR'S EVE I had an invitation to a party at Bill Astor's house—around the corner. He is Lady Astor's son and is about thirty-five. There was also a party at our Officers Mess. The evening was organized thus: Mess party from 9 to 11; Astor's from 11 to 1AM. I had Maxine Birley for the evening—she is said to be the best-looking girl in London and we attribute her looks to being half Irish. The Mess of course had the best orchestra in London. Good old American swing. We had taken over the grand ballroom of the largest hotel in town, where one thousand officers can eat at once; there were about five hundred couples at the dance. All the girls managed to find evening dresses and it was quite a cheerful, pre-war sight. A beautiful long bar on the balcony, and lots of seasonal decorations. We had a good time watching everyone and dancing; Maxine being very much the top-drawer little English lady could tell exactly which girls there were "nice" and which were ordinary, regardless of their clothes or make-up or jewels or anything—this from almost any distance, too.

At eleven we went down the street to Astor's where everybody was very social and very rich and knew all about each others' private life, which they would discuss with anyone. Since I was the G-2 Duty Officer on call for the evening, I had to call HQ and let them know where I was in case the enemy chose to help us celebrate New Years Eve, but nothing untoward occurred. Was safely in bed by 2 AM up at 8 AM, long enough to report a quiet night, and back into bed all morning, as I had the day off.

✦   ✦   ✦

21 March 1944

THE OTHER NIGHT we met lots of the neighbors, finally, when some fires got started in the vicinity of our flat. Everybody dashed out with buckets and stirrup pumps, and we discovered that we had some very amiable neighbors, one even offered to wash our window curtains for us, as she knew we had no maid.

Every evening now we must attend an officers' refresher course. This goes on for two weeks, and re-instructs in all of the basic military subjects. I must say, the military creed does all that any set of principles could do, and possibly human nature isn't quite up to its demands. For it could produce all the best things in a person, but also it can beautifully camouflage a phony, or butter over the lazy. We are in the process of trimming down again, as once before, and everything has to be ready to operate at a moment's notice in any way. Maybe that is why Goering is getting busy, even in such a feeble way.

❖ ❖ ❖

30 March 1944

WHATEVER GEN. MONTGOMERY says is all right with me. Of course, this would be the case by military law even if it were not my personal wish, but it so happens that in this case both coincide, and if he ordered me to attack the Siegfried Line with a sling-shot I would quite willingly do so, because I would believe that whatever caused him to give the order, would cause the result to come right, provided I did everything that could be done with a sling-shot. And since yesterday, 29 March, I will not listen to anybody who says he is anything but a great man.

A staff meeting was called for 10:50 AM in a certain theater near HQ. Monty arrived at eleven, so in the interim I had time to sketch the stage scenery that just happened to be set up that day. It was presumably for some ballet or other. On the wall over the fireplace was a large sketch of a female in a pose indicating an air of abandon if not downright you-know-what. One might almost have expected the Commander-in-Chief to arrive from the wings in one great leap accompanied by a crashing chord from the orchestra, and to proceed with a choreographic interpretation of "what to do with the Germans." But soon in he came, his beret on, and one page of paper in his hand, a small figure but one you'd recognize anywhere and at any distance. He took off his hat, laid it and the paper on the table and proceeded to chat with us in a pleasant, informal way about the job to be done. There were no slogans, no proclamations, no sentimentalities and no boasting remarks about the 8th Army (of which many English complain) but instead, a calm lecture full of good sense. I was left with the impression that he is perfectly sure of what he is about, and untroubled by the size of what responsibility he carries just as he is unconcerned about the credit for the inevitably successful outcome. (The British think of him as a publicity seeker, but I happen to know that he is pressed by various Ministries to make many public addresses for purposes of civilian morale.) He spoke for forty-five minutes, then said, "Well gentlemen, I won't keep you from your work any longer. Thank you." And off he went, just as unassumingly as he entered. It was particularly interesting to hear the chatter in the hall; one recognized accents from all parts of the Isles, and all parts of America, and even from the other Allies, as we are truly a combined HQ in every sense. He stressed our allied complexion and told us we are to think of every action we take as it might affect our allies; here is the only sort of place where allies really are alike, in the face of a great event. And even then I know exceptions, but they are all people who will never be great. An ally is not something you are given, it is something you have to work for, and there are plenty of obstacles in the form of jealousies, suspicion, ambitions and differences of background. Some Americans still think this is the Revolution of 1776, and our enemies the British. And some British are insufferably conceited, stuffy and insular to the Americans, but the younger generation—captains, majors and lieutenants—are learning the lessons that will count in the future in the way of cooperation, and that, I think, is what matters.

✦   ✦   ✦

Easter Sunday night

THE CHURCH THAT I attended on Easter Sunday was over a thousand years old. If you have a map handy, it was near St. Albans, north of London in the little feudal-type Hertfordshire village of Great Gaddesden. The local squire is Sir Wm. Halsey, the vicar is Edward Halsey, and the assistant vicar for the service was Capt. Thomas Halsey, who has the small job of commanding the battleship *King George V*, the heftiest unit of the British Navy. The service began with Alleluia, just as at home, and another old hymn of the same type, but then they sailed off into those unpredictable liturgical chants that delight the Episcopalians and go on and on till they are singing whole paragraphs of Scripture on one note. A brief rather crisp sermon helped. The Church itself was partly made of field stone and flint and reconstructed here and there with cement, but it had the old boys in plaster and halos under every archway and in every dark corner, while gargoyles were about to take off from ledges around the ceiling and undressed cherubim made ready to sock them with chipped and worn harps. The organ was good and the decorations excellent as spring is very lavish in this part of the world. After the service I met the battleship skipper; he complained that the U.S. Fleet would probably sink all the Japs before he could get his craft out to that neighborhood.

❖ ❖ ❖

21 April 1944

IT IS TIME TO re-consider affairs.

1. Anne. [my sister] She is both well and provided for by George. Therefore, those being the two considerations I had in mind in 1942, I do not think it necessary to make any specific allowances out of my insurance. The principle is, should my insurance become valid, you do what you want with it, making Anne a present of whatever seems wise after any pressing matters are met.

2. Based on nothing more than that she has been a good friend and musical companion, I should like Decima Knight to have a flat 250 pounds sterling, which would be a lot to her, and she has always earned her money the hard way. I admire her for it, and therefore wish to make her a present.

3. Take care of Ma Demarest without any mortgage consideration, out of the insurance.

4. Make a present of a helpful sum to Aunts Helen and Jane. Otherwise I don't see the sense of making a lot of complicated arrangements

with a mere twelve or thirteen thousand or whatever it is. If I were you I would abolish your mortgage. The very thought of 51 Mt. Ave. being under mortgage irks me.

Actually I do not expect to meet with any particular disaster on the Continent, but it's always well to have some last words written somewhere just in case. Should correspondence lapse at all, it should be no cause for concern. There will of course be some confusion, inevitably. And in the bustle there might be little time for writing. But nobody is to worry. With my usual ability for getting into odd situations, I have succeeded in finding the Army's most interesting and least typically military job.

✦ ✦ ✦

7 May 1944, Near Southampton

I HAVE LEFT the sinful city and rejoined the B&LS (Brutal and Licentious Soldiery) in the field. This is not a change of job; it is merely the first step towards Berlin. General Montgomery has the great honor of being my boss for a while, but as you can imagine, it was only after long and careful deliberation that I reached this conclusion, or rather this dispensation. Since it seems that Monty is being opposed by his old sparring partner, Rommel, the first few rounds of the fight ought to be of absorbing interest. Rommel apparently does not know that I am also opposing him, as he has made some very cocky speeches lately, but he is being spared that nasty surprise till the last minute.

Since June 1942, I have watched the sun's path stretch across three seas, the Atlantic, the Irish and now the English Channel. The Atlantic was rough, tempestuous, boisterous, the kind of sea that should surround a new world, that only an adventuresome soul would try to cross. The Irish Sea was a deep blue border of a kind of fairyland peopled by elves, goblins, damsels in castles and Druid ghosts. Somebody painted the Irish Sea and put it down between England and Ireland to give the prosaic English the right setting for an occasional trip to Never-Never Land, which Ireland is. And now the Channel, full of secrets, watched on both sides by every kind of weapon man has been able to think up, its waves practically weighted down with mines, pieces of airplanes and ships and sort of holding its breath a little longer now than it was. Even so, at evening on clear days it has an air of peace and that same golden carpet stretching westward. Gosh, you will think I have nothing more military to do than sit on the beach and dream up descriptions. Well I have, but the ocean always gets me.

I am living in a drafty old house right smack on the Channel coast, with a group of English officers. They are all young, intelligent and well-traveled. The sort of people who tell each other jokes in foreign languages. The day starts with a soft-shoed orderly bringing you a cup of tea at about 8 AM. I'm sure this will be the case even in the heat of battle. Incidentally, I wangled some Nescafe from a friend and have trained my orderly (called a batman) to bring me coffee instead of tea. Breakfast for the Englishmen is between 8:30 and 9:30, but I can't wait that long and have a habit of getting up a bit earlier than the rest in order to take a slight walk along the shore before eating. Everybody works in shifts, but the officers are more or less always on duty. After breakfast, each toddles off to his respective job. At 10:30 there is a clamor in the back driveway as the W.V.S. (local matrons) roll up with tea and pastries, and work pauses for fifteen or twenty minutes. Lunch comes at one, a rather lavish tea at 4:30 and dinner at 7:30. I must say, the way the day is broken up by pauses for refreshment somehow sets a very even pace to everything. They work later, true, but more steadily than Americans do. Slower but steadier. There are villages at hand where the natives hold dances quite regularly. You can imagine it's fun to be the sole Yank here. Altho I've been down here only a week or so now, the usual form is: "I say, America, will you play the piano for us?" They always call one "America," when they don't know your name.

I had better mention that I am in another one of those out-of-the-way places as far as mail is concerned, and mine may be delayed in reaching you as well as vice versa. Packages have been arriving nicely and are very much enjoyed by many people. The best piece of mail yet is the picture of you two sitting on the front steps. It's not only a good likeness but it brings back so many things to my mind—among them the fact that if I were home right now I'd be sitting on the steps leaning against the opposite pillar enjoying the sun just as you are. By the time I can do that again, I hope to have very well earned the right to—how, I don't know yet. It's a wonderful picture. You haven't changed, but it vexes me in a way to think that after all the years in which I may have finally gotten some sense into my head, I should have to be this far off and try to commit everything to letters. One forgets half the things one intended to include when the letters are written.

✦ ✦ ✦

29 May 1944

IMAGINE THIS. EVERY morning, at about 7:30 AM, the door of the room (or tent flap, wherever one happens to be) is gently pushed open, and in slinks an individual, soft-shoe style, who in dulcet tones announces that a cup of tea awaits one, inferring "as soon as one can rouse ones self sufficiently to take it." Then this body disappears as swiftly and as silently as it came, taking with it one's shoes to be shined. One then stretches forth one's hand till it connects with the cup of tea; this all requiring a minimum degree of consciousness, but the beautiful thing is, that as soon as some of the tea has gone down, one awakens speedily and achieves a state of sociality and coherence that could hardly be imagined by anyone who had not experienced it. This practice, I hold, is the answer to all getting-up-in-the morning problems, and if I acquire no other luxury in life, I shall strain every resource to provide myself with a body who appears in the morning with ye olde cuppe, and I shall never worry about possibly being morose, taciturn, or misogynic if this ritual is followed.

Mind you, it is only in the English HQ that such a thing happens. These very civilized people have learned the sense and wisdom of it. U.S. HQ still stumbles out at dawn and goes thru various barbaric customs like exercises! of all things and parades, before breakfast. How to shorten life. I hold that you can get just as much done if it is tackled more deliberately.

7

France

ON JUNE 8, 1944, two days after D-Day, I crossed the channel with the 2nd British Army under General Dempsey, and was based with them at Bayeux near Gold Beach; Juno and Sword being the other British beaches. The Americans were on Omaha and Utah beaches to the west. As a signals intelligence liaison officer, I was stationed with the British for almost two months, but I was officially assigned at that time to the U.S. 1st Army under General Omar Bradley. With two superiors, British Brigadier Williams and American Brigadier General Sibert (Bradley's top intelligence officer), I moved between the two tactical headquarters. I must say, I thoroughly enjoyed the hospitality of the British Army headquarters for the reasons I recount in some of my letters home.

When I arrived, the British beaches had been largely cleared of the enemy, and the freighters were beginning to arrive with supplies, tea, and equipment for the next event. There was not as much carnage at the British sector as there was at the American. The chief action had been on Omaha Beach. There, the American Army had some three thousand casualties and had lost large quantities of equipment due to German fire. At one point, General Bradley had had to consider seriously whether to withdraw. The other American beach, Utah, to the west of Omaha, had been quickly taken by the Americans and became the base for the liberation of Cherbourg and Brittany.

Progress was initially slow and costly as the Allied forces fought to clear the Germans out of the Normandy area and advance southward. It was the British mission to hold the attention of the Germans in the

Bayeux-Caen area, while the Americans advanced from Normandy to the base of the Cherbourg peninsula, turned left and headed eastward for Paris. Well, it wasn't quite that easy. It took until mid-July for the British to take Caen and for Bradley to reach St. Lo. By then the Allies were positioned for the breakout from Normandy. Bad weather stalled the support aerial assault until July 25th, my twenty-ninth birthday, but when it happened it was impressive—over twenty-five hundred Allied planes dropped about four thousand tons of ordnance on the German targets identified by our intelligence. This massive bombing allowed the Allied ground forces to finally break through the German lines. It also wiped out a visiting general from the Pentagon who wanted to see what real war was like and got a little too close to it.

Through our signal intercept services, we learned that the Germans were planning a mighty effort to cut us off at Mortain and prevent us from moving east. This advance knowledge of the German intentions allowed the American forces to be prepared for the German attack. So prepared, in fact, that Winston Churchill himself traveled down to Avranches and Mortain to watch the fun.

We knew the Germans were afraid of General Patton, and for this reason he had earlier been used as an effective decoy stationed with his troops in southern England to convince the Germans our invasion would take place at the Pas de Calais. Patton believed in reincarnation, and thus reluctantly accepted this assignment as he did not want to go down in history as just a decoy while someone else became the real hero. The ruse worked perfectly to deceive the Germans all the way up to Hitler himself, as we learned from our later intercepts of German communications. Now Patton was in France for a real attack on the Germans that would open the way to Paris.

The methodical Germans attacked on schedule and the Americans were ready to meet them on the same schedule. General Patton, completely informed of the enemy's intentions, helped crush the German attack at Mortain. The rest of the German Army was transfixed by the presence of the British up north in the Bayeux-Caen area. This kept a large part of their army out of the Avranches and Mortain action. Historians still argue about who gets the credit for the Allied success in these battles. I, of course, would claim that signals intelligence saved the day.

About this time there was a shift in the high command. General Bradley took over the newly formed U.S. 12th Army Group that included the 1st Army, now under General Hodges, Patton's 3rd Army, and me as a newly minted major on his G-2 staff. Once I began moving with the American Army as part of Bradley's intelligence staff, I continued as liaison officer between our own G-2 intercept detachments on the front lines and the British detachments under our care slightly to the rear. Enjoying the confidence of Bradley, Sibert, and the British, I moved around freely, often at my own initiative, wherever necessary to fulfill my role. I must confess, it was impossible to know where I would be or what mission I would be engaged in at any given moment. You might say I played the war as I played the piano—by ear. I would visit our radio operator detachments, positioned as near to the front lines as possible without risk of capture; move between U.S. and British Army headquarters; fly back and forth to BP; and generally stay on the move. My duties necessitating this movement involved keeping track of German communications, overseeing radio operators in the field, trying to find out what the Germans knew about us, and most important, trying to read and analyze their intentions for the immediate future and pass on that intelligence promptly. All of this against a background of the beautiful landscapes of the French countryside, the gratitude of the French people at being liberated, and the internal comforts of Calvados, the neighborhood drink of Normandy.

Once through Avranches, the American Army moved rapidly toward the Seine in pursuit of the retreating German forces, only remnants of which ever made it back to their homeland. What had initially been a slow, costly advance by the Americans through the Normandy hedgerows became a rush toward Paris. With the rapid retreat of the Germans, they had little time to send radio messages and our local signal intelligence activities dried up considerably. By now, Bradley's headquarters was moving almost daily, as was I. This pace never slowed until we got to Verdun. But first, we had a parade.

On the morning of August 25, 1944, General Leclerc's French 2nd Armored Division entered Paris, the first Allied force to do so, followed closely by the U.S. 4th Infantry. An enormous victory parade up and down the Champs Elysees ensued the next day. As a tribute to American-French relations, the French Army was given the lead position in an exuberant procession that included all participating Allies and, of course, General de Gaulle, who liked leading parades. With almost twenty thousand Germans still in Paris, lots of fighting took place even while the celebrating was going on. The French have always been good at combining these two activities.

I then conducted my own reconnaissance of Paris as my driver and I toured the city streets in our jeep, accepting the plaudits of the French along with bottles of wine, bunches of grapes, and grateful kisses from both men and women. I particularly recall this event through the manifestations of gratitude offered by a French Catholic nun whom I in turn, out of my gratitude, parked in the back seat of my jeep. This picture was especially pleasing to the Parisians, who love kissing. Yet one could not miss hearing gunshots, as the Army wiped out nests of German snipers and the French dealt out summary justice to known or suspected collaborators or anyone else they did not happen to like at the time.

We were not allowed to stay in Paris very long. Had we done so, the war would have come to a complete halt because of other distractions. But under the direction of General Bradley, General Patton's 3rd Army and the 1st Army to the north under General Hodges moved rapidly eastward toward Germany, keeping up the momentum of our victorious advance. Somewhere in this massive movement of troops and equipment, I had a place in a jeep with General Bradley's staff. The race across France, in pursuit of the Germans, came to a halt in the famous French fortress city of Verdun where the main headquarters of

Bradley's 12th Army Group were established and I found myself finally in a place to rest.

When the Germans took over a French village, they would commandeer their own lodgings, often at the point of a pistol. This was hardly necessary when the Americans rolled into a town. The French were eager to welcome us into their homes as the following personal story will attest.

I happened to stop at the gateway to a home of a local French businessman who waved me down to ask if I could help him take his child to the hospital for medical attention. I was only too glad to comply, and in return he offered me the freedom of his household as long as I stayed in Verdun. This was about a month. The child was taken to the hospital in my jeep, recovered, and the family was ever afterward equally grateful both for this event and for their liberation from the Germans. They were also overjoyed at my occasional gift to them of Nescafe and American chocolate, to which they responded with some of the best French cooking I have ever experienced. It far surpassed the American officer's mess. The child's recovery somehow reminded me of my own experience at the age of two, when for unexplained reasons, I too was allowed to recover from what could have been a fatal illness. So perhaps, I have returned the favor.

On another occasion I performed a favor that I know was long remembered. Tooling along a country road near Verdun, theoretically pressing the German departure but allowing them the freedom of the road ahead as I was but one jeep and they were considerably more at that moment, I came upon two weary French lady cyclists to whom I gave a lift home. One was the organist and the other a singer in the local church, so I stopped to join them in song. I recall writing out one of my favorite hymns for them on an old brown paper bag. Twenty years later, when I was an officer in the Foreign Service, I revisited eastern France where I found myself on a long hill near Verdun leading to the small village where, in 1944, I had given these ladies a lift. I found their church—it was empty and cold. I climbed up to the organ loft and there pinned to the music rack was my piece of brown paper. The notes were still legible. Going into the village, I made inquiries about the organist and, alas, she had passed on. Everyone knew of her and of the American who had been there during the war and written out some music for her. The priest had made the American an honorary member of the parish. It was not for me to reveal my true identity. In so doing, I would have interfered with the growth of a legend, one that fulfilled all the essential elements in the French imagination and which each villager shaped to suit his or her own fancy. For me it was, and is, a lovely memory, brought to life each time I hear the notes that I know are written on a piece of brown paper pinned to the church organ in a tiny village in eastern France.

As you will read in my letters from France, there were other such memorable and pleasurable encounters as I made my way across the country with our armies, which the French called their "liberators." The war in Europe continued in a series of encounters as the Germans retreated. The Allied high command mistakenly began to assume that the Germans were defeated and about to give up. In this frame of mind, we established our main American headquarters in Verdun, close to the border of Germany, and our forward (or tactical) headquarters to the north in the ancient city of Luxembourg. Unfortunately the Germans were not defeated at that point, but this is jumping ahead of the story.

8

Letters from France

TRAVELING WITH THE British Army during my first two months in France gave me ample opportunity to experience their military lifestyle and to describe my observations in letters home. Since my duties continued with intercept intelligence, I couldn't write of my war work. Instead my letters convey the flavor of every day—camping out in the fields, scenes of the countryside, and meals shared with the locals—as well as the extraordinary day I drove into liberated Paris. In particular I tried to capture the incongruities of the situation, such as a placid cricket match being played while a fierce dogfight roared overhead. It may well be that the necessity for observing and gathering non-military material to write to my parents helped hone my intelligence skills. Well, in any event, they knew I was alive.

❖ ❖ ❖

20 June 1944, France

COULD YOU BUT see, you would find me in a pleasant field surrounded by hedges and poplar trees and well-camouflaged "things" (cannons) of military significance. Not so far away a continuous rumble shakes the ground even here; Monty is having a serious altercation with somebody. This morning, as we were organizing tents, etc., a soldier reported a booby-trap in the field. The Major went for a look; there, just sticking out of the ground an inch or so was the white tip of a shell or bomb of undeterminable size. The Major acted. Ordering everyone to a safe distance, he grabbed a mallet and (from a safe distance himself) threw it at the shell tip. He missed on this and the next ten tries. Finally one well-aimed throw headed right for the spot, and everybody ducked with ears full of fingers. Crunch. Instead of a shattering concussion there was only the sound of an egg-shell breaking; what we had thought was a nicely planted ticket to Kingdom Come was only a half-buried egg that the Germans had been unable, in their hurry to get out, to consume.

My impression of war in France was strictly from "What Price Glory" and "All Quiet on the Western Front." Rain, mud and shell-holes. Well, our first day here was in that tradition. There was rain, there was real mud, there were shell-holes. There were traffic jams and great big trucks stuck in ditches. There was a colorful air raid in the darkness as we were disembarking. The minute the Englishmen got away from home they all started using the word "bloody" to describe everything, this being a disreputable cuss-word in polite English society. Those wonderful persons, the cooks, suddenly had most tempting odors issuing forth from the most improbable places and one was given enough calories and vitamins to face a campaign right up and down Mt. Everest and the North Pole instead of mild, moist Normandy. We had no sooner reached our destination when up came the first dispatch rider with the company mail. Of all incongruous touches! Artillery rumbling on the horizon, bombers overhead, solid lines of military traffic, and here, in a French field, I am greeted first by the Maplewood News, the church bulletin and your letter with the picture enclosed. Also, *Time* has arrived and helps a great deal in these circumstances. What service.

We do not know just yet what is writeable, so there isn't much in the way of news.

✦ ✦ ✦

27 June 1944, HQ 2nd British Army

ONE CERTAINLY FINDS oneself in odd circumstances, composed of the most contradictory elements, in a war. For instance, we have our dining table set up under some trees, and a loud-speaker connected with the company radio is fixed up on one of the tree branches. Today a particularly heavy barrage was going on at lunch-time; at the same time the radio was giving us the NBC symphony orchestra playing Tchaikovsky's Sixth, three cows were grazing about twenty yards away and a Spitfire patrol swept round and round overhead. Sometimes the artillery came in just like tympani drums, perfectly timed for a passage in the symphony, and sometimes the Spitfires swept over low enough to join in a big crescendo. Meanwhile the cows munched on unmindful of all, and the ten or twelve officers at the table did the same.

Having my laundry done has become quite a pleasant affair. There is a French family in the village—typical middle class well mannered chatty people—where the Madame insists on doing the wash without pay if I provide *du savon* which of course I can well afford, plus a few bars of chocolate or some Nescafe. Instead of just leaving the wash, it is now the custom to stop for "café-noir" at a proper after-dinner hour. A colleague and I bring the coffee and Madame inevitably produces a delicious Spanish-cream sort of dish to accompany the coffee. They relate experiences with the Germans and seem to have more respect for the Germans' behavior than for that of the local French who sold all their produce to the Germans and later went around even removing boots and clothing from German corpses and selling these objects at very high prices to other French. This type of Frenchman wore German colors in his lapel, and then when we came quickly changed his colors like a chameleon and appeared with the Allied colors.

Some of the villages are ruins; some are perfectly intact. Bayeux looks just the way it would in peace time. Not a scratch. Restaurants are even open. All kinds of troops are there, and the worst behaved I think are the Canadians. They have very little discipline, and while they are wild and ferocious in the front line, they fail to conceal these traits when in normal surroundings. I wouldn't be without a pistol in a Canadian-occupied town.

Three of us have constructed a very solid and comfortable dugout. The Germans not being so very far off made it advisable. We dug down about four feet, then built up the sides and roof with logs. These logs had been used by the Germans as obstructions in the fields to prevent Allied glider landings. We took the jeep and using a tow-rope dragged the logs from where they were stuck upright to our hole. We feel quite secure in this dwelling from shells and things dropping from planes, rain and wind. Every night we brew up some soup or Nescafe on a sterno stove and have some crackers and Isigny cheese. The latter is particularly good, and can be bought in the neighborhood. Sometimes the orderlies turn up with white or red wine. I have saved some cans of tongue and ham that you sent, and these are a welcome treat, which we use a little at a time.

Occasionally, at mealtimes, a small boy and girl come around with a pitcher of fresh milk and pour into each cup, in return for which we fill their pockets with hard candies or chocolate from our rations.

If things are slow for a while, we take cautious walks around the countryside, which, incidentally, on a clear day is quite beautiful in spite of all the military things in it. You actually see very little military. It's all concealed, dug in and tucked away. The only obvious things are road traffic and the ceaseless patrols of fighter aircraft.

There is absolutely no sense in your giving yourselves any concern for my safety; I feel infinitely more safe here than I ever did driving into N.Y.C. on that sky-highway. But alas, I can find no piano in the village.

❖ ❖ ❖

30 June 1944, 2nd British Army

CONDITIONS BEING WHAT they are, a rainstorm here is an occasion for the entire camp to suddenly appear totally undressed and proceed to take a natural shower bath. It is effective and practical but cold. And often we are caught all soapy when the rain decides to stop. This is really a dilemma. The weather changes so quickly that one has to be fairly nimble about this type of bath.

I am getting pretty tired of the sound of airplanes. Hate to think of listening to them forever. They spoil the peace of the countryside!

❖ ❖ ❖

8 July 1944

ALTHOUGH I SHOULDN'T write any details of D-Day, I can say that for those of us who knew it was to be, the atmosphere was something like the night before Christmas. All preparations had been made, of course, and it was only a matter of waiting on the weather. Our evenings were spent in card games and song-fests. Everybody went to bed early on the night before D-Day, and everyone was up when the first air fleet passed overhead on the way to bomb the beaches. I've never seen such a terrific sight as the sky-full of planes that appeared that morning. They were quite high and seemed to hang in the air while the earth moved past them. It was a good clear morning and everything could be seen distinctly overhead. The roar seemed to fill the entire universe.

I didn't leave England until a few days later. I went on an American LST (landing ship tank) which looks something like a tanker or Great Lakes freighter. In the middle of the night our bow doors were unfastened by the heavy seas and began to slam back and forth with each wave. This shook the entire ship. We were forced to leave the convoy and sail back to England, where we changed ships and set forth on another, in calmer weather, with good sunlight and food and berths in the crew quarters which all reminded me of the old cruising days minus the orchestra. This time the trip was completed without incident until we reached France, where there were multi-colored lethal fireworks about which I think I am not supposed to write. Anyhow it was fun, and we had a grand rest in the good care of the combined British-U.S. Navies (mostly U.S.).

The other day I drove up to Cherbourg. It seems to have been a military necessity to bomb certain towns out of existence, but as we passed thru them, the French had the bravery and forgiveness to cheer us and wave and smile standing in the heaps of stone and glass that had once been their homes. It was more than touching. In Cherbourg itself delayed-action explosives were going off but nobody paid much attention. The town was not as crushed as it might have been; only the important structures were demolished. Aside from the remains of towns, the Cherbourg peninsula on the western side is quite beautiful countryside, cut up into many colored patches of field and woods, the latter with chateaux established on small hill-tops in the best tradition, but all on a quaintly miniature scale.

I am having a fine time, living most healthily, spending no money at all (my expenses are met with chocolate, salt, cigarettes and gum) and talking a glib and polished Francais. Hope some mail is getting thru to you but be patient and don't worry.

✦   ✦   ✦

14 July 1944

YOUR DESCRIPTION OF Maplewood on D-Day is interesting. "Inward" excitement is hard to picture. I think that there was a general feeling of anticlimax all over England when the Luftwaffe failed to appear and there were no signs of the imminent end of the world. To me it all pointed up the vicious habit the newspapers have of building up public tension over something; if it weren't D-Day it would have been the price of mutton. And to find in France a crowd of frightened Poles, willing Russian deserters and poorly equipped Huns instead of the mighty Wehrmacht behind a mountain of cement—it was a bit of a let-down. Of course I don't mean to minimize the difficulties now, when they've brought up some real soldiers and opened up with their V-1 buzz-bombs. It won't be a short affair by any means. And from what we know of the actions of the German SS boys, if there are any left alive after the war I will be surprised. They are most unpopular.

This afternoon we had a good show. A flock of German fighter planes had the nerve to fly over this sector. We were having a quiet conference, when the sudden wallop of the surrounding anti-aircraft artillery woke everybody up. We went outside just in time to see a Spitfire and a Messerschmitt doing a very tight turn, the Spitfire chasing the other. It was a clear sky and we could see it all most distinctly. Just as they completed a circle, smoke began coming from the German; he turned over and the pilot fell out, while his plane dropped to the ground and exploded. Just after that, another Spit suddenly came dashing up underneath another Jerry, shooting away, until the Jerry pointed his nose straight up, hung vertically in the sky, and then fell to the ground. Each time a polite cheer went up from every field in the vicinity, where the earthbound were watching in little groups. It was something like watching a tennis game. There were far more Allied planes around than German, so it was all rather one-sided.

We are camped near a river, so the problem of how to wash one's head no longer exists. On sunny days we take towel and soap, and go to the bend in the river where a large tree grows out over the water. Here it is deep enough to dive and swim about. One gets wet, climbs up on the tree and there, sitting on the branch, gets good and soapy, then you dive in again, and later, dry off in the sun on the river bank. Almost any sunny afternoon you would find us there, naked warriors all, like a scene from *l'Apres Midi d'un Faune*, while dog-fights go on upstairs and the usual artillery rumble continues over the ridge to the southwards.

Speaking of that ridge, my curiosity got the better of me yesterday and I went over it myself, to see what lay beyond. I can only look at a hill so long, without having to get over it and see the other side. On the other side of this one was more beautiful rolling French countryside, but there was a kind of poison in the atmosphere. The fight had been going on quite recently there, and much evidence was scattered around. The sight of so much ruin and the smell of death begins to mean something different when you face it freshly done than when you see it months old, as the ruins in England. Yet still, the natives wave, those who are left. I had a look at Carpiquet Airfield, from which Jerry used to take off for England, and the retribution looked like a scene out of the Old Testament.

The owner of a cornfield nearby lives in a chateau and it contains a rather thin sounding piano. His wife is quite musical and has a large library. There are two very good pianists in our group—chaps who can read Bach, and Beethoven sonatas right off. Many evenings are spent thus at the chateau, until dark, as there are no lights and the noise begins, anyhow, at nightfall.

Paula, our laundress, and Camille, the older woman who lives with her, today had a tea for one of the Englishmen and myself, in honor of its being Bastille Day. Paula, being of Russian parentage, is giving some of our boys Russian lessons, some French lessons and some German. She turns our chocolate bars into puddings and our biscuits, ground up, into pastries. She also repaired my sweater, after I had fallen into a thorn bush with it. This is all very convenient.

✦   ✦   ✦

27 July 1944

ONE THING I have definitely acquired in France is a better understanding of how to play Bridge. I never had a very clear idea of what the scoring was all about, but now I do. The usual routine is for our game to begin in the dugout at about 9 PM. We are just finishing the second rubber, as a rule, when the Germans come over to do some kibitzing. This in no way interferes with the game, but has just come to be accepted as a routine thing and in fact serves to wake us up if in case the cards have been dull. Last night my partner and I made rubber in two hands. The first two.

Sometimes the Germans also come over to watch our cricket matches, and a fine dog-fight will develop overhead but the stately minuet goes on undisturbed. I think cricket is a good game for very hot days, as there is a minimum of fast movement required. It is also a good occasion to catch up on one's reading. I have seen Americans play cricket and get some of the baseball spirit into it—speed and a bit of noise as well. As the English play, it is most astonishing to see a person catch a fly and hear a polite round of applause sweep over the field; or, if he misses, hear everyone murmur "hard luck, old chap."

On the night of my birthday an impromptu gathering developed at which there appeared a bottle of something called "Calvados." I cannot pretend that it is exactly a soft drink. It is a native product made from apples, but is water-colored and about as hot as brandy. We had a pleasant bull-session. Oddly enough, we had the most fun recalling scenes from Marx Brothers films—all these Englishmen were properly ridiculous and like the Marx Brothers as much as my brother John and I do.

While amongst the English, I have been giving talks to the soldiers on events in general. This practise was more likely to be done by an American than by an English officer because, I think, the Americans' attitude is more democratic as far as the soldiers are concerned. However, most of the English officers now agree that it is a good thing. The Canadians are of course like the Americans in this respect. They take great pains to see that the soldiers are well informed about the battle and the world in general. The English have the opposite instinct by nature. Yet from the questions the soldiers ask after a talk, one can see that they are interested, reasonably intelligent and beginning to wake up. There is not nearly the same gap between American officers and soldiers as there is between the English.

Your letters of 22 June and 18 June have come thru all right, but I'm perturbed that mine have not reached you, as I have written quite regularly since D-Day.

Incidentally, I have talked with a few Germans and find them pretty glad to be captured!

I have told Decima that she may consider herself engaged, which she has accordingly done. (Don't ever tell her I put it that way!) She sings me songs over the BBC from England. She is twenty-three, a good cook, a good sport and loves to sing for people at gatherings, which is a good antidote for my natural reticence. She is best at light opera things, rather than jazz. This forces me to become a better sight-reader.

❖ ❖ ❖

3 August 1944, G-2 Section, HQ 12th U.S. Army Group

Such is the state of affairs in our part of France now that I don't expect to get any mail till Christmas, if by then. Everything is moving forward at great speed, and while it is a fine thing in every other way, it is too much to expect that the post office would keep up with the rate of advance. Moreover, I have had such a variety of addresses in the past two months I'm sure nobody knows who or where I am—or didn't until I arrived at the above location, where I hope to stay for a while.

The first thing I will do upon rejoining an American officers' mess is gain back the weight that was lost on British rations. Life at British HQ is a succession of small snacks, none of them amounting to very much, and the heaviness of their puddings is the factor which serves to keep one from getting hungry for long periods. Of course we have been on so-called "field" rations, which consist of a succession of stews and endless processions of soda-crackers. But even field rations at U.S. HQ are varied and appetizing.

The roads around Normandy are getting more piled up now with German wreckage. Of course we don't go fiddling around with it looking for souvenirs or useful bits, as the Germans have all kinds of tricks with explosive results to surprise the curious.

I am beginning to cuss at the old brass hat back in Ft. Dix who ruled that we couldn't bring cameras. Of course, all the later troops had all the cameras and film anybody could ask for; it was only the early contingent that came under that rule. There are plenty of scenes worth taking, but I will have to store them up in my head.

At an English HQ one is awakened at about 8 AM by an orderly who brings a cup of tea and takes one's shoes away for polishing. At American HQ one wakes up at 7 to a bugle, and one goes to breakfast without any help. The English are so much older in their ways than the Americans that the present scene resembles an overgrown boy scout camp by comparison. But the breakfasts here are so good that I'd get up at 5 to eat them if I had to.

At the rate things are going I expect the Germans to fold up soon. What happens then I can't imagine.

❖   ❖   ❖

4 August 1944

OUR STORY OF the week is of a dejected, dirty, fed-up German prisoner, who when asked who he was, answered, "*Ich bin V-2.*" (V-2 is supposed to be the German's next secret weapon.) He hadn't lost his sense of humor but most Germans start out with no sense of humor to lose.

The chateaux, which the French build, are even more spacious and formal than some of the English country houses. They always have beautiful tree-lined avenues leading to the courtyard in front, and little "witches towers" perched on every possible corner of masonry—pointed affairs just like the drawings one sees in books of fairy tales. Of course the peasants houses are just the opposite, and there is no "in between." It's either a palace or a hovel.

I now work for General Bradley and he is very well. Am now a Major. Have been since August 1st, although I just found out this morning.

◆ ◆ ◆

10 August 1944

Y OUR LETTER OF July 12 arrived today stating that you finally received my post-D-Day letters. Well that's a relief. You now know that everything is fine. To my way of thinking, the war is much more difficult when one is far away from it than when it is just around the corner. And it is safer in France these days than it is in London.

The greatest change has been August weather. The woods, the cool nights and the clear practically sparkling air all remind me more of Eagle's Mere than anywhere else. Luckily I have accumulated a sizeable bedding roll, and have not yet minded any night air, however cool.

No other news. Of course you notice that our present successes coincide with my rejoining the U.S. HQ!

◆ ◆ ◆

26 August 1944

Y OU SAY YOU can't imagine me in the surroundings I describe; sometimes I have the same trouble. Yesterday I was driving around the countryside looking for places to put things and it was nearly 10 PM before I was through. It was rather flat country, with low and rolling hills and patches of wood visible for miles around. On one horizon the twin spires of a famous cathedral dominated the landscape, making quite an impressive sight in the dusk. Foolishly I had come out without my bedroll, but I didn't think the job would take so long. It was a good 120 miles back to my tent, and blackout driving is no fun at all. While I was wondering what to do, a thunderstorm appeared out of nowhere. Then I suddenly remembered that not far away I had passed a farmhouse where the people had seemed particularly friendly and amiable in their greetings as I drove past. It was about a mile or two away, but with a drenching rain, thunder and lightning there was only one thing to do, particularly when one's only shelter is a jeep. I drove into the courtyard of the farmhouse. Cobblestones, as usual, surrounded by barns, lofts, stables, and on the roadside, the family house. The daughter of the house appeared. I asked if there were room for me overnight; she led me to her mother, who said of course, and without a second look at my rather dripping garments she stirred up the fire, slapped a large piece of beef in a pan, brought out some apple brandy and red wine, and a loaf of bread as long as my arm. Meanwhile Monsieur appeared, as did Pierrot, his eight year old, and Claude, about five. And a dog named Bobbie. The daughter, about nineteen, I guess, was named Thérèse.

We sat in the kitchen, and chatted and sipped. I had my dictionary with me, so the talk went fairly well, and I even got as far as teaching them yes, no and o.k. At 11 o'clock (which is only 8 o'clock to the French), I decided to turn in. Madame showed me my room and the *cabinette*. I think they gave me their best bed. I was most comfortable with good linen and nice rugs—all a great contrast to the kitchen. And the first sheets since London.

I woke up to all the usual farm noises, chickens, pump handles, cartwheels, horses, etc. But, this being wartime France, I was hardly prepared for the breakfast. Thérèse appeared, and asked if two eggs would be enough for breakfast, or did I want more than two! (The Army never serves more than one, and hardly ever that.) There was also coffee and toast. When it was time to leave, I offered to pay them, but they wouldn't accept anything. Instead, I emptied my pockets of cigarettes, chocolate, crackers and everything else I could find, all of which

I carry as much for this express purpose as any other. And I promised that when I came back I would bring some soap. I left at about 9 AM, much refreshed, and made the trip in daylight and in comfort.

The scene at present is undoubtedly one of the most peaceful in the world. I am on a hill overlooking a river, and in the near background are all the familiar lines of a French town. The countryside has probably been just like this for a long while, for everything seems to have grown into its place, and become adjusted to every other feature near it. In the town are all kinds of flags, and across the streets are banners saying, "You are Welcome" and "Welcome to the Americans." Some of the U.S. flags in house windows are quaint but rather touching; they have a profusion of oddly arranged stars, any old number, and the number of red and white stripes also represents the family's best guess; but the impression is genuine and you can tell that Madame and Mademoiselle have spent a good deal of time sewing it all together. All the little children have been taught the most engaging manner of greeting. Today at the main corner a little seven-or eight-year-old girl was going from car to car, at each one stopping, handing the driver a big ripe red tomato, doing a curtsy, blowing a kiss and going on with her basket to the next. Every town gives either tomatoes or apples to the convoys passing through. And every country inn and farmhouse has something that the Germans never discovered, which they have saved for the occasion; that is, wine and eggs for us, and the carving knife for any Germans hiding nearby.

Did I tell you I was a Major? In French I am *Le Commandant*.

◆ ◆ ◆

1 September 1944

YOU REMEMBER MY overnight visit at the French farmhouse? Well, shortly thereafter I moved into the same vicinity, and of course went back to see them. They got out a nice fat chicken, some delicious but unnamable hors d'oeuvres, beans, pears, apple tart, red wine and soup (not in the order named) and we had a fine dinner one evening. Of course another thunderstorm came up just at about 11 PM, so I stayed the night, being unable to resist the temptation of a good bed as opposed to a cot in a pup-tent in a damp patch of woods.

A few days later little Pierrot took sick. This distressed Madame Baron because the doctor, who lives in Chartres, had no gasoline for his car and there wasn't even a way of advising him of Pierrot's condition. Luckily I had a jeep, and not to suggest that a very long detour was necessary, managed to pass the doctor's house where I stopped, gave the news, had coffee and cognac with the doctor and his mother, very good people, returned to the farm with the doctor and after he had seen Pierrot, brought him back to the city. I went to the drug store, got the necessary medicine and that night took it to the farm, where both M. & P. Baron were of course much relieved. It looks as if Pierrot might have diphtheria. I was very glad that we got the Dr. there when we did. It's fun to drive up to the Baron farm; the little kids come running out on the cobbly courtyard shouting *"Bonjour*, Robert," but M. & Mme. always observe the form, and say *"Bonjour, Mon Commandant,"* and ask if I'd like some cider or an egg.

I have found the real *Cathedrale Engloutie* in fact, after having known it for so long in Debussy's music. A while ago I had occasion to come down the west side of the Cherbourg peninsula at about 5:30 in the morning. At Avranches there is a hill, from which one can see out over the Baie de Mont St. Michel, and there in the distance, half hidden by mist and the half-light of early morning, was the Cathedral of Mont St. Michel, coming right up out of the sea and so perfectly fitting the music that I could hear every note as I watched. I am sure there is a picture of this in the encyclopedia; get it and you will understand exactly what I mean. I stopped there in Avranches and had breakfast. Meanwhile the sun came up and lighted up the cathedral until it looked exactly like a diamond with the sea as a setting. Later I drove out to it. The cathedral itself is right at the top of the island, which itself is a mere pile of rock. Below the cathedral is an entire town, living in circular tiers and very close together, about 250 permanent residents, and tiny hotels with room for some two or three thousand tourist visitors. Way up in the highest part of the cathedral was a sweet French girl of nineteen years, named Marcelle, who told me she'd been there ever since 1940 without going to the mainland. She was selling cards and pictures of the place, all by herself, in an enormous high-ceilinged room. She wanted to get back to civilization, naturally. I left there and wandered around town a bit, then pushed off to the mainland. I half expected to see the Mont gradually disappear into the sea, with Marcelle like an imprisoned fairy waiting to be rescued from the last visible turret. The effect of the image plus the music is overwhelming and turns the piano score into an orchestration almost automatically. I hope you can find a picture; I have lost my postal cards in the general shuffle.

I suppose I am permitted to say that I was in a certain city on the day of its liberation. That was fantastic. The French are volatile enough, but combine this with their cultural liking for Americans, plus the fact of four years of repression under the Germans, and you get a rather picturesque welcome. All the approaches thru the suburbs were lined with waving, cheering and (if one had to stop in the traffic) kissing French civilians. Bottles of wine were placed in the jeep, tomatoes, bunches of flowers, everybody wanted something autographed, and cigarettes, which the poor people hadn't had for so long, almost started riots. In the city it was the same thing magnified many times. I once found myself giving a speech of welcome to about five hundred people who just seemed to gather around when the jeep stopped at the side of the street. I said we were happy to be in France, and the American people sent their best regards. This was very well received.

Of all things, they had carts selling water ice, and three policemen came up with three dixie cups full of it, all of which I felt obliged, in the interest of international amity, to eat. Then they offered to guard the jeep while I was taken into a café for some glasses of wine. This could have gone on indefinitely, but there was still some shooting going on and I felt it might be better to leave in the daylight. So I buzzed off. You will not think me careless or opportunist to have kissed quite a few very good-looking Parisiennes who seemed inclined to express welcome in that particular manner. They seemed surprisingly well-dressed, and the proportion of women to men was about ten to one. Ah, war. But more of that when the rules permit.

We are now living in open country, camped under apple trees that are beginning to ripen, so that the apples thud on the tent roof all night long.

Since we are doing a good deal of moving around, I do not have as much time to write but will try as often as possible.

◆ ◆ ◆

7 September 1944

AT LAST I am learning something useful! My teacher oddly enough is my driver, Page, a Kentucky boy about the same age as myself but completely "unspoiled" by city civilization. He owns a small coal mine in the Kentucky hills, hires sixty-two laborers, and would rather hunt and fish than anything. Tinkering with motors comes next on his list, and he is a reliable and punctual driver. What I am learning from Page is how to fish with a safety-pin and some string. It happens that my tent stands on the edge of a pond, with the open end facing the water. There are weeping willow trees leaning over the water, and some very mellifluous bullfrogs live just under the bank. Page knew there were fish in that pond just by the way it looked, and in no time at all he had a safety-pin out of my sewing kit, and neatly bent it into a fishhook shape with his pliers, had a nut from the jeep as a sinker, a cork from one of my brandy bottles as a floater, and a worm as bait. He fixed up a willow branch for a pole, and the operation was complete, except for some fish, but we expect them to recover from their surprise soon and start nibbling. Meanwhile any evening you care to drop in you will find me encamped and sitting on the bank before my tent with an undisturbed fishing line, possibly a hook, and undoubtedly a small touch of good French cognac. The water will be as calm and clear as a mirror, the evening sunlight sparkly and the countryside peaceful, except for now and then a disturbance when a mine gets run over in a field or somebody locates a sniper. An extra loud boom means that the bomb disposal squad has piled together a lot of mines they've found and let them off all at once. The only thing General Bradley ever said that I heard on the detonation was a casual, "What the dickens do you suppose is going on over there?" and he went on about something else. Last night we had a violent thunderstorm and the pup tent swayed and slatted, but never weakened, and I slept very well and securely.

Summer has disappeared with hardly a bow. Today we have the typical Northeaster; everybody is drenched, the wind roaring, all hands in gloves and legs in long woolens. Still the pup tent stands. Nearby stands a chateau, where dwells an aged Comtesse for whom I chopped some wood which I also enjoyed in the form of fire. She is very "old world." The first thing she asked was, am I an officer or not. Then she asked about my family. Our maternal family name Des Marest made rather a good impression. I am clearly "acceptable" now. I must ask her more about that name.

General Patton came in a few nights ago. There were two soldiers snoozing on the grass near where he stopped his car; they were the drivers of two jeeps nearby. In the jeeps were two Colonels waiting for Gen. Patton. I watched the Colonels jump out, approach the General, and one introduced the other to Patton, who thereupon noticed the soldiers. "Who are they?" he asked. "Drivers," answered the Colonels. "Well they're soldiers, aren't they!" said the General. "Introduce them too. They're just as good as any officer in the Army." Whereupon a red-faced Col. introduced personally two very surprised privates to a Lieutenant General, and all were then satisfied.

By some queer coincidence one of Gen. Patton's assistants is a Lt. Col. Allen, of the famous journalist team of Pearson and Allen, who originally broke that story about the slapping. Figure that one out.

Another colleague around here is Major Ralph Ingersoll, the publisher or rather newspaper editor. The Lt. Col. next above me is a partner of Carter Ledyard & Millburn. Another is a former Dartmouth professor of sociology. My immediate boss is a Brig. Gen. E. L. Sibert, from Martha's Vineyard and Farmington, and he is as excellent a boss as I have ever had, one who gives me complete backing, appears to rely on what I say and is most friendly when we have the chance to sit around and talk. If I ever met with an accident, I should want you to inform Gen. Sibert that he was an ideal guy to work for.

❖ ❖ ❖

13 October 1944

I HAVEN'T BEEN able to write for a week or two because of frequent journeys between which there have only been short breathing spells. It occurs to me that I should give you a list of the names of French people who have befriended me and gone out of their way to be nice, so that when the civil postal service opens up you could send them some small token from you and me.

Enclosed is a picture of Murian, the country place of Baron Chadenet. The other day while buzzing down a country road in my jeep I passed four wee tots on their way home from school. This was a temptation—I love to fill the jeep with little kids, so I stopped and in they climbed, so excited they could only squeak and giggle. It turned out that they lived on the Baron's estate, and as we drove up the driveway a lanky, bony figure in tremendous plus-four knickers disengaged itself from the lower branches of a walnut tree along the side. It was Baron Henri, with his mouth full. It soon developed that he could speak English, and that I could speak French, so we did a reverse play, each using the other's native language, and each glossing over difficult words by the convenient dodge of having a mouth full of walnuts. We were the first two Americans the Baron had seen, or any one else there had seen, in fact. My driver and I "liberated" them, over several glasses of cognac and with much handshaking. The Baron had acquired a Russian farm hand who had escaped from the Germans, but who could speak no French. I found myself in the droll position of translating a Russian's German into French for the Baron, who would reply in English. The Baron was deeply concerned over the question of American–Russian relationships, so when I shook hands with the Russian and declared that I was certain our countries would always be friends, the Baron was hugely pleased, and invited me back to lunch the next day. Our conversation was interesting, for, as a contrast to my Chartres friends, Baron Henri is a staunch Royalist, and doesn't pretend to know what the "people" of France want. He wants a King and a good army. But he did admit that De Gaulle seemed to have all factions behind him at present.

A bit of business developed the other day whereupon the General ordered me to take a plane immediately to London, which I did via Paris. A couple of hours to Paris in a Piper Cub—what a way to see France! It was a gloomy day, raining sometimes, so we flew along the ground. At Paris I got into a respectable plane and went to London. There I saw Decima for a few hours Sunday morning, but had to come right back. Stayed in Paris overnight, where the only untoward incident was a loud and near explosion, later reported to have been a German V-2 rocket. Paris now is like London used to be. Swarms of Americans, but very little damage to the city yet. Lots of things to buy, if one wants to pay. I did find one good item which I sent home. Hope it reaches you.

Gen. Bradley has a lot on his mind lately, especially as the war seems to be stretching out again. He sometimes seems to be a little impatient with the British, but otherwise is even-tempered, unpretentious and well. He said today that he was fed up with this inching forward bit by bit. That kind of war doesn't suit him at all. Or me.

9

Luxembourg

ONCE THE MAIN headquarters for the 12th U.S. Army Group was up and running in Verdun, I moved with General Bradley's staff to his tactical headquarters in Luxembourg City. I had a small office there in a commercial building right at the end of the main bridge of town. Going to work each day was just like going to the office in New York, with one notable exception—the frequent visits from German bombers. Once again, my duties as intelligence liaison officer had me on a heavy travel schedule between Bradley's tactical headquarters, the British headquarters under General Montgomery in Belgium, and Verdun.

Our G-2 Section received all intercept material from Bletchley Park and American sources relating to the European Theater, plus other intelligence data. It was my job to boil it all down, synthesize it, and get it to the commander. On one occasion I was privy to some sensitive German intercepts that laid bare the worldwide spy network run by the Vatican and revealed many diplomatic secrets of both the Axis powers and the Allies. Here is what happened. One day three GIs came into my office carrying a large heavy waterproof wooden black box. It was about six feet long and three feet high. They had found it at the bottom of the Schliersee, a lake in Bavaria, while dragging it for the body of a drowned soldier. They did not know the content of the box, but in line with their duties, they brought it immediately to high headquarters for intelligence analysis. With some effort, we pried the box open. The contents were well preserved and turned out to be volumes of German intercepts of the Vatican's wireless traffic with all of its church outposts throughout the world. The Germans had been monitoring this traffic and translating it into German from Italian and Latin. Word spread quickly around headquarters of this discovery. There was great sensitivity to the diplomatic implications that could well involve high politics and religion. Thus, when word of this chest (which was sitting under my desk) reached the State Department representative at Bradley's Verdun headquarters, it was instantly commandeered by the diplomats and disappeared from us in a flash. I never saw it again and have never heard it referred to in all my experience with the government and the military. I can understand that the State Department did not want to acknowledge this treasure—somebody did not want to embarrass the Pope. There has been no reference to it in the history books, in the annals of the war, or memoirs of the generals. I can only say that had I had the time to peruse these German intercepts, they would have probably provided one of the most fascinating reads of my war experience. And the least reportable.

At first our days in Luxembourg had a certain routine to them, and we had a great deal of social contact with the local population—attending dinners and gatherings. But this activity contrasted dramatically with the atmosphere in the city once the Battle of the Bulge began. Then, the residents took down the American flags, closed their shutters, and waited for the worst. We, on the other hand, were instructed to "display confidence." This was not just a pithy bit of advice; it was an order. Do it. Now, an order to march or to charge the enemy, or to fire the torpedo, is easy to carry out; you can perform the act as ordered, or you can have ample time to regret it if you do not. You have been trained to do it, and when the time comes, you do it without question. But an order to display confidence calls for obedience on an entirely different level.

General Ike's order came about as the result of the following circumstances. The scene was Luxembourg, December 1944. The snow lay deep on the countryside and in the forests. There was little visible military movement on either side. It appeared that the Germans were inclined to let the Christmas season pass without bloodshed. There was silence along the front. Some of us noticed that the silence was more profound because the German military wireless system had shut down. On December 12, one of our detachments intercepted a German order to all units to observe total wireless silence from then on. All German radio traffic abruptly stopped. Perhaps the Germans had become suspicious. It could not have been more obvious to those of us in signal intelligence that a storm was about to break: the absence of Enigma messages, rather than their presence, told us that. Of course, this immediately dried up "food" for the hungry machines at Bletchley Park. I reported the matter to General Bradley and warned of the sinister implications of the situation. He, however, did not seem unduly alarmed and issued no alert. There were other clues, too, that something big was about to happen—aerial reconnaissance had noted increased vehicle movement by the Germans, but these signs were misread or ignored as well. In the chaos that followed the December 16 "surprise" attack, we took some eighty thousand casualties that, in my opinion, could have been largely avoided had the radio silence order by the Germans been correctly interpreted. I warned General Bradley that he was about to be surprised. He was.

The Battle of the Bulge caught the U.S. Army completely off guard. General Ike was in Versailles at Supreme Allied Headquarters when the storm broke, and General Bradley was on his way to meet him there for a meeting. I was in Luxembourg City having a quiet game of bridge with Kay Summersby, Ike's driver, and two fellow officers. The quiet was interrupted by a phone call from the duty officer at the command post. His terse message: Tiger tanks and fifteen German divisions were on the move in our direction. The front was in confusion, and nobody could tell what was really taking place. Kay dropped her cards and immediately departed for Versailles. I headed for my duty station at General Bradley's headquarters, there only to find that the orderly's report was all too true, and the American 1st Army in Luxembourg was in a state of near panic. Because my particular responsibilities included ensuring the safety of our Ultra communications link with Bletchley Park, I immediately phoned the British detachment and advised them of the situation. I suggested rather than ordered the British code detachment to down tools and head for safer territory. The reply was, "Oh, no sir, we are just having tea, and we have to finish that before we take any action. Besides, we have seen you Yanks panic before, and it always comes out in your favor in the end. So please calm down, and we will continue with our tea." The British were right. I calmed down, and their tea went on undisturbed. I felt we were lucky to have such allies.

The next few days, however, were chaotic. Ike himself was practically in confinement against a rumored assassination plot. American units at the front were overrun, and they surrendered. Buzz bombs began to appear in our area. German parachutists dressed in American uniforms were dropped behind our lines to sow confusion. The weather, always dark and cold, turned worse, and our Air Force was grounded. At one point, a small military force unit and some staff officers were all that stood between German armor and our forward American command post. We carried pistols.

It was about this time that an order appeared—"Officers will display confidence." I could not understand the order. Was I to have confidence and show it, in spite of the facts, which were not such as to inspire it? Or was I to display confidence because presumably the generals knew what they were doing and one could assume that all would soon be well? General Eisenhower had called a meeting in Verdun of the commanding generals of the First, Third, and Seventh Armies along with certain staff members, including me. General Ike sat in the head chair. There was an air of uncertainty in the room. The overall impression was that we had been caught with our pants down, in a tactical maneuver that the Germans had been pulling in every war since the time of Frederick the Great. Ike turned to Gen. Patton: "George," he said, "what do you think we ought to do?"

From that point on, it was pure theater. General Patton, a great officer but also a great ham, rose to the occasion. He took the floor and in a splendid military oration traced the history of battle crises all the way from Alexander the Great to George Patton.

"I'll have 3rd Army up here in three days," he said, "and we'll kick 'em in the ass."

Ike said, "That's impossible."

Said George, "I've already started."

Patton did, of course, make it to Bastogne in three days. But he had some help. The weather was one of our worst enemies until Patton ordered his chief chaplain to pray for better weather. The chaplain complied. On Christmas Eve in a small local Protestant chapel at a service led by General Patton himself as parson, with the German Army about four miles away, appropriate prayers were offered and heard. The very next day the weather cleared completely, to the satisfaction of General Patton and the Air Force, who came out in full strength with both supplies and ammunition and an aggressive state of mind. This was our Christmas present to the Germans. I believe General Patton gave the chaplain a military medal for his effective performance. The staff of Twelfth Army Group, which constituted Patton's congregation, felt a new sense of confidence and refreshment of spirit.

And once the Germans broke their radio silence, which of course was necessary to instruct their advancing units, our intercepts revealed their objectives (chiefly Antwerp), their order of battle, their formations, and who were their commanders. Their radio traffic spread the whole plan out before us: we knew how strong they were, where they were headed, and what they hoped to accomplish. The only trouble was that we were a little late in finding all this out.

Somehow, in the midst of this crucial battle, a memorable musical opportunity presented itself. The front lines were about twenty miles away, where the Battle of the Bulge was in full cry, with German buzz bombs overhead coming from the north. I was walking along a street in downtown Liege in Belgium, in pursuance of some duty or another, when my eye caught sight of a door standing ajar. Beyond the door, I saw the black and white pattern of a keyboard.

Aha. The Germans could wait. At all cost, I would have to possess that keyboard, if only for an hour. Putting aside all thought of house-to-house fighting, I crossed the threshold and approached the target, an upright piano of ancient vintage but still possessed of all its keys, like slightly yellowed teeth, and two pedals turned a bit inward like pigeon-toed feet. I pride myself on being able to coax sweet sounds out of any piano. Here, indeed, was a challenge.

Presently, I became aware that the room, although poorly lighted, was not unoccupied. Several girls were very quietly lounging around—as if waiting for visitors. A feminine voice inquired, in well-modulated French, as to what my business might be and how it might suitably be accommodated. A toss in the hay was the furthest thing from my mind, although I believe not from hers. But I asked only for permission to play the piano for a while—a request that was readily granted, along with a glass of beer. I played the same concert I would have presented in a hometown auditorium, or at a Garden Club luncheon. These *filles de joie* had similar and well-educated tastes. They wanted Gershwin, Cole Porter, Rogers and Hammerstein. I even offered Liszt, whose "Liebestraum" I thought might enhance the ambiance in which they made their wartime living.

A constant parade of soldiers entered by another door, marched upstairs, attended to their needs, and marched out again. I wondered how many of them, or of us, would be alive twenty-four hours later. In that one battle in Belgium and Luxembourg, we took eighty thousand casualties. The enemy took even more.

After a few hours of music, I returned to my post of sterner duty. But there was a message—would I please play the field organ in the morning for a service of the Anglican Church, led by the British military chaplain? This I did, conscious of the wide and all-encompassing nature of my various audiences. As Harry Truman once commented: he didn't know what was going on upstairs, he just played the piano. In my case, upstairs meant heaven, as many of us would soon find out. But I felt sure that once we got there we would meet again those kind, lovely girls who in the middle of a very dark night, invited me to play their piano and share their hospitality—and never mind whatever else was going on upstairs.

They just wanted some music. So did I.

❖   ❖   ❖

Two weeks into the Battle of the Bulge, when the American Army was reeling back before the surprise onslaught of the Germans on the American headquarters, we began to make preparations for a withdrawal from Luxembourg City back into France. The German advance was moving rapidly. In some cases, our troops held the line and in other cases they retreated. But the retreat gained momentum, and soon the Germans were about four miles east of Luxembourg, moving steadily toward the American tactical headquarters.

At a morning staff conference, plans were announced for a withdrawal and volunteers were asked to form a rear guard for the destruction of sensitive material and equipment. No mention was made of how the rear guard was to get itself out of there. The Germans were coming down the road with Tiger tanks, and our rearguard was armed with .45 caliber Colt pistols. This did not seem like much of a match. So we resigned ourselves to whatever the future held. I volunteered to be a member of the rearguard along with fourteen other brother officers, and we supplied ourselves with extra pistol ammunition. Nobody knew how to operate any weapon of larger or more dangerous potentiality. Those were anxious days. I was designated one of the last-ditch detachment, and I prepared to do battle with my .45 against any German tank that showed up. But none did. They must have realized the formidable opposition they faced.

As events turned out, our troops east of Luxembourg held the Germans, and the uneasiness at headquarters gave way to confidence in our safety. I did not have to face a Tiger tank with a pistol; I did not have to write a hasty will for my heirs; and I did not have to make necessary plans and arrangements for an imminent demise. I did not have to exchange my life for the protection of materiel or documents. All these things had passed through my mind but due to the valor of the front line infantrymen in the dead of winter, with bazookas and other lethal weapons, I was not called upon to make a last stand like General Custer before the onslaught of the Indians. Signal intelligence people, including myself, were not supposed to be captured, for fear of the enemy finding out about our biggest secret. But I did not even have a cyanide pill.

As the Battle of the Bulge wound down, the Germans had a farewell greeting for us in Luxembourg City. They operated a huge cannon mounted on a railway flatcar that, during daylight, they hid in a tunnel. At night, along about 3AM, they would push the cannon out of the tunnel and aim it in the direction of our HQ billet in the city. The idea was to wipe out General Bradley's entire staff with a lucky or well-aimed shell. If this failed, they at least could ruin our night's sleep, which they did on a regular basis. Our signal intelligence detachments had the capability of tracking the direction from which incoming artillery was coming, and this they did with some precision. Thus the site of the railway tunnel was pinpointed, to the great delight of U.S. and British fighter-bombers who, after a good breakfast one day, took off and closed both ends of the tunnel, entombing the cannon and all of its crew. The tunnel actually caved in. From then on our sleep was undisturbed. Having played its last card, the German Army began to disintegrate and its leaders began to provide for their future by surrendering and seeking favors from those they had just been trying to kill.

10

Letters from Luxembourg

FOR OBVIOUS REASONS, while located at General Bradley's tactical headquarters in Luxembourg City my letters home did not give my location. Not until after I was assigned to help the G-2 Section of the 9th U.S. Army in Belgium, could I write where I was and had been. There was much to preoccupy us at that time and my correspondence was less frequent. The German escapades in the Ardennes provided good material, although I felt a rather light presentation was in order to reassure my parents all was well with their son. Only later, when I returned home, would they read the citation I received from the 12th Army Group for a Bronze Star Medal with Cluster and learn what I had been doing:

> Major Robert E. Button, Signal Corps, for meritorious service in connection with military operations from 1 August 1944 to 1 February 1945. As chief of the Signal Intelligence group in the G-2 Section, Major Button's contributions to the successful operation of this section were considerable. His special knowledge of signal intelligence combined with that of German Order of Battle, enabled him to act as an authoritative interpreter of German Army movements and intentions. His extensive knowledge, clear thinking and good judgment were such that he was solely responsible for determining the causes of an apparent security breach in our communications, the discovery of which in time undoubtedly resulted in saving many American lives.

8 November 1944

EVERYONE IS GROUSING about the mail lately. Either there is so much coming from U.S. that the post office is swamped, or the transport facilities are busy with other things. Anyhow, we aren't getting much, so morale is very low indeed.

As a counter-measure, we had a ball. The local Duchess could not come, as she is still in England. But General Bradley and all the others came and danced with all the sweet young natives. It was their first grand ball in four years—we had one native orchestra of about twenty-five pieces, mostly strings, and the American orchestra of about fifteen, mostly brass. The native orchestra was perfectly continental to the epaulettes on the leader's uniform, and they played Viennese waltzes, polkas, corny continental folk dances etc., while in contrast the U.S. outfit played our own folk music a la Glenn Miller. There was champagne, ice cream, cookies and cognac. I had the prettiest girl in the place, and everyone conceded this fact. She speaks English, French, German, and the language of this country, which is a mixture of all three and her name is Madeleine Arendt. Photo enclosed. She works as secretary for a local official of some kind.

We have just received the election news. I suppose you voted for Dewey. I would have been very sorry to see him elected, possibly because from Europe Roosevelt appears to be a greater statesman, and everybody in Europe looks up to him. Dewey's speeches did not strike me as being of presidential caliber. I voted for Roosevelt and for Republican Senators and Congressmen.

I regret very much to report that the usual PX Christmas shopping routine was not made available to us this far forward; therefore unless some friend can do some work for me in Paris, I shall not be on hand with presents come Xmas. However I have already sent some perfume to Mother and Anne, I hope it arrives before it all evaporates or breaks or gets stolen. Bought it at Guerlain's in Paris last month. Any other purchases there were foolhardy. The war has been forgotten completely. It is politics and money. Prices are astronomical, every American is a target, and from all I hear, French Parisians have resumed their former ways with even greater vigor, if possible. Many people, French and American, believe that when we leave, or if we leave, France would not hold together, so serious are the political factions and so well-organized are the Communists. In fact, the Communists seem to be about the one strong party in France, which could easily lead to trouble with Spain, as so many French Communists are itching to "get" Gen. Franco. The war is going to last a long while.

I am very well but would like to be sitting in front of the fire in the living room instead of here.

❖ ❖ ❖

25 November 1944

THANKSGIVING DAY HERE in [censored] was called "Yankee Day" by the local population, and has been adopted as a national annual day by the country we are now in. All of the civilians who could, invited soldiers to dinner, and in the evening the officers club had a band concert to which all the officers brought the civilians who had been their hosts. The Prince came and caused much excitement. The natives are very proud of him.

But at dinnertime on Thanksgiving I was in a car in Holland, in a pouring rain. In fact, I was not aware that it was Thanksgiving at all. I had made a trip to Brussels by plane, then, in view of the weather, to Holland by auto. I had to get back here that night, but the chances of taking the plane back from Brussels seemed slim. My pilot was a cocky little sergeant named King. He said we could try it, but we might get up and find ourselves completely in the fog, or we might get nearly home and find it impossible to land, then it would be too late to turn back to Brussels. Anyway, we decided to try it. There was a good railroad we could follow all the way. We took off at 3 PM, into a dismal, murky, threatening sky, with a drizzle of rain and a fair amount of cross-wind. King turned his cap around backwards—that's what he does when he really is working. We set off about two hundred feet over the railroad tracks and hoped for the best. Brussels disappeared in the mist. Now and then the tracks disappeared but we found them by going even lower. We came to Namur, and when I saw trains below at the station I envied the people anchored to such a steady, tangible (and warm) contrivance, while we bounced around as if someone had us on the end of a string. After Namur we began to hit mountains, where the tracks ran thru valleys and we were below the tops of the hills ourselves. This was the worst part. It was then too late to turn back to Brussels, and the horizon on all sides seemed to be closing in on us. King would now and then fly around in a circle, to avoid some fog, or just to wonder what to do next. He always decided to try to go on a little further. We did, always seeming to be headed right for the thickest murk, until we came to the end of the mountains, where suddenly a speck of sunlight appeared. Then off to the west the sky became clear and a beautiful, a broken-up mass of clouds and rainbows and sunlight spread out ahead, while behind it seemed to be darker and angry to have let us escape. Believe me, I didn't have any turkey dinner, but that moment made it a Thanksgiving day for me. King put his hat back the proper way, and grinned, and dived at two cows in a field just for relief. We got home just at dusk. Maybe I've got a new grey hair or two after that one.

◆ ◆ ◆

2 January 1945

A LITTLE LATE, I admit, but I wish you both a Happy New Year, and we will assume that the next one will see us all in the same place. Christmas and New Year almost slipped by unnoticed in the turmoil of the second half of December. Up to the 16th everything was fine, people were stocking up for Christmas and the enemy wasn't paying too much attention to us (we thought). We had our first snow here, and everything looked lovely, with the many musical church bells in the vicinity filling the air all day long with Christmas sounds. Our war maps had a secure aspect, with some question marks but nothing very startling on them. The officers mess was planning a Christmas party.

On the 16th, some queer rumors began to trickle out of the Ardennes. Civilians became apprehensive; they are scared to death of the Germans, because all during the occupation they refused to accept German nationality, which irritated the Germans beyond words. They said to us, you don't know the Germans, they are like lice, when you kill one, a hundred others appear. The Americans seemed too complacent. On the 17th the complacency began to evaporate. I will never forget it. A dark, snowy, gloomy day, the air force grounded, the atmosphere menacing, rumors beginning to multiply, planes in the night carrying parachutists to our rear areas, peasants appearing on the roads from the north with stories of burning villages and German tanks on the loose, and then the sound of artillery beginning to increase in the not too great distance. The civilians looked at us with a mixture of anger and worry, and they started to remove their Allied flags from the windows. The war maps suddenly began to look alarming. The generals were delighted that the Germans had come out into the open, but not being a general, I saw a lot of things to worry about and I think I lived thru a great deal of 1944 in the short space of a week. All the same German tricks were being used. Agents were causing traffic jams, others in American uniform were trying to create panic on the roads, German tanks were being reported in the most unlikely places and the most fantastic stories of all sorts were being circulated. There were even mysterious telephone calls passing alarming reports. And every day got more murky, more oppressive and more mysterious.

Things having come to this pass, I went to my room and dug out a small Irish lucky piece which has always brought me good luck; this I put in my pocket and concentrated my thought on good weather for the air force. I happened to be duty officer at HQ on what was regarded as the most critical night, and I acquired about two dozen new gray hairs, indigestion and a cold that night, waiting, as I really thought possible, for either German tanks or parachutists, or if not these, just for daylight and breakfast. The Irish luck piece worked wonders. The next day dawned without a cloud in the sky; in a short time our air force was all over the sky, the civilians began to unpack their belongings again and the Germans began to lose tanks. The snow glistened for a change and the whole aspect of things changed. For five straight days the weather continued thus, and you must have read about the results. It took me those five days to get over my cold, but I still have the new gray hairs—at any rate I feel they were honestly earned.

Christmas whizzed by, but I did have an excellent dinner with a local family to whom I gave one of the pounds of coffee, which you sent—thank you very much indeed. A local housewife would have to pay $30 for a pound of coffee if she could get any at all. Another pound I gave to the family of my two Maquis friends near Sedan; they were tickled pink and immediately called in about ten neighbors for a cup; I am known as the *Liberateur* of that tiny village, by virtue of having been the first Yank to drive thru. They wish my picture to put up alongside of de Gaulle's.

✦   ✦   ✦

13 January 1945

THE AIDE TO THE Chief of Staff is a major named Bob Shackleton, who used to sing in N.Y. and has a good baritone with which he regales the assembled officers of the 12th Army Group HQ while I provide the accompaniment. We can go on for half an hour now without music and without stopping, since we know all the same music. The brother officers seem to like our efforts and we enjoy ourselves immensely, whether we have an audience or not. There are some good arrangements with modulations into different keys all the time to make them interesting; we have about equal musical instinct and usually tend to interpret songs similarly. So if we have to sit in Germany or anywhere for very long, such activity should prove most refreshing.

A party including Clare Luce and a host of junketing Congressmen dropped in with their attendant photographers; their main concern was in keeping Clare from getting all the pictures taken of her, but she at least is pretty, while the others gave very little evidence of having that which you're supposed to have if you're not pretty. Life must be dull in Washington. We had no packages from Jerry while the visitors were here, as Hitler undoubtedly appreciates the harm he could do our war effort if he were to eliminate any Congressmen.

Winter is beautiful here, cold and dry and crisp.

❖   ❖   ❖

5 February 1945, Belgium

W E WEREN'T ALLOWED to say so, but we have been in Luxembourg for quite a while and all my letters for two or three months have come from there. Only when I had left could I use the name in letters. It certainly was a pleasant, old-world, picturesque country. I have sent you some pictures of it, a book about the liberation of the country, which was given me for a Christmas present by my Luxembourg family, the Arendts. Madeleine, or "Madely," the daughter (as usual), wrote the inscription on the front of the book. I took her to local dances.

Once I flew over to London on business, and had dinner with the Leith-Ross family. Sir Frederick is head of UNRRA [United Nations Relief and Rehabilitation Administration] for Europe, and was trying to get some insulin to Luxembourg to help a current wave of diabetics. I was going back next day, and had General Bradley's personal plane, so I offered to get the insulin to the Prime Minister of Luxembourg, and in fact, delivered it just two and a half hours after I left Sir Frederick's house. Thus I was able to do the Luxembourgers a favor. The Prime Minister was delighted.

Luxembourg City was a happy place until Old von Rundstedt [head of German military forces] decided he wanted to come back. But we never moved out withal, which imparted great comfort to the populace and is a fact of great credit to our General. The Germans were not far away, as you know. If we had pushed off to somewhere else, the people might have become panicky.

The piano is being used more and more lately. The other nite we had a small song party at which the best performer was one Russ Forgan. He is a colonel, and does a very good Al Jolson type act.

While I was in London, I took Mr. Birley a bottle of Benedictine. He had just finished a portrait of the King. Had I been ten minutes earlier, I would have been in time for tea with just Mr. B. and the King, in his studio. The Benedictine made a great hit, as not only is it worth its weight in gold in England, but it is Mr. B.'s favorite liqueur. His house had just lost its windows from a nearby buzz-bomb.

◆ ◆ ◆

7 February 1945, Belgium

F<small>IELD</small> M<small>ARSHALL</small> M<small>ONTGOMERY</small> came down here to lunch the other day, and General Eisenhower turned up too so it made for lots of saluting and comment amongst the retainers about Ike's new five-star shoulder insignia. It consists of a circle of stars; otherwise, if they were in a row, like ordinary four-star generals, they would have to hang one from his ear, or give him a zoot-suit uniform with extra-padded shoulders to accommodate all the rank. Monty made a bet with my boss, General Sibert; he wrote on a card "Field Marshal Montgomery bets General Sibert that the war in Europe will be over by 1 August '45. Signed B.L. Montgomery." The amount was five pounds. Actually General Sibert believes the war will be over much sooner, but he thought that even if he lost the bet, the card would be worth considerably more than that so how could he lose.

✦   ✦   ✦

28 February 1945, Holland

YOU WILL IMMEDIATELY understand the current success of the 9th Army when I tell you that I have been assigned to it for its present undertaking. Without going into detail, which I can't, there arose a need in a certain place for which I appeared to be qualified, thus I have switched addresses again, and country and language as well. I know no Dutch at all. But most of the natives speak French, fortunately. The Dutch seem to have built very prim looking towns in their flat and dreary country, and they give a very contented-middle-class atmosphere, in contrast to the feudal snobbishness of Luxembourg, the grubby industrial bustle of Belgium and the oxen-cart pace of life in rural France. The Dutch girls, however, are not the slightest bit exciting, as a rule. They do not quicken the atmosphere around them, tho undoubtedly they purify it, as opposed to what the French do. And of course, the tidiness of Dutch housewives is perfectly obvious everywhere. One thing I like about Dutch towns is the custom of having the church chimes play tunes for two or three minutes every half-hour. It makes pleasant listening in the night, when you wake up.

Here and there I am getting some clues as to what to do in the post-war world. Ralph Ingersoll gave me one. His backer, Marshall Field, is gradually going more and more into radio. Ralph opined that Marshall Field would be more my type of boss than David Sarnoff. Ralph has some interest in radio himself. I might tie in with that combination. Hint number 2: General Sibert has offered me an introduction to his friend Julius Holmes, one of the President's aides, a member of the Clayton-Macleish-Stettinius etc. group now making foreign policy. Or, said the General, military intelligence is seeking to build up with some young men. It appears that the Army is in competition for talent with private business. While I am being so disgustingly boastful, I may as well tell you this; I am no longer Major Button, Signal Corps, but instead, Major Button, General Staff Corps, which is a promotion in dignity if not in dough, and occurred last week.

The next letter will be about other people.

◆ ◆ ◆

March 1945, Namur, Belgium

BELGIUM IS A SMALL country, with odd-looking houses with panes of blue glass and yellow gables, and huge fortresses built into the mountains. It rains all the time and the streets have not been cleaned in the towns since the Middle Ages, if then. Exception noted: the Ardennes country, where the German push went, that is quite beautiful. I have driven up and down the Meuse Valley and some of the scenery in the mountainous regions is tremendous. It's hard country to fight in, but would be perfect for either summer or winter vacations. Complete with chateaux, hunting preserves, ski slopes, gorges, wild boar, and lots of snow. But the rest of Belgium, no thanks. Once General Bradley told me he would rather have stayed in Luxembourg.

11

Germany

Early 1945 saw the collapse of Hitler's Germany. After the Battle of the Bulge, in which they lost two hundred thousand men, most of their remaining aircraft, and all of their strategic reserves, the German Army retreated to its homeland with the Allies in close pursuit. The next four months of warfare was one of overwhelming Allied forces pitted against an ever-dwindling resistance of fanatical SS units and diehard German soldiers.

As with every war (except in Ireland and Palestine), the shooting winds down and something resembling peace descends over the scene of hostilities. In these circumstances the job of the intelligence people becomes that of finding out what the enemy may have had in the way of future plans had the outcome been different, and what the enemy knew about us and how they knew it. This was the mission of the Intelligence Target Task Force of which I was now director. To support this new mission, I was provided with a staff of twelve officers and sergeants; air, land, and sea vehicles; and complete carte blanche on where to go and when. Not bad for a draftee turned major. While officially now part of General Simpson's 9th Army G-2 Section, my area of operation covered all of Western Europe. My letters describe my enthusiasm for the task and some of what I encountered on my investigative travels. One week I might be at 9th Army Headquarters in Brunswick, the next perhaps investigating a munitions plant in Nordhausen, and the next meeting with folks at Supreme Headquarters Allied Expeditionary Forces (SHAEF) in Frankfurt. To SHAEF headquarters were drawn all the business prospectors, historians, scientists, carpetbaggers, sociologists, would-be politicians, art dealers, journalists, and manufacturers from the world round, looking after their own interests and futures. Our task force supplied the intelligence, or raw material, to facilitate their search.

On secret airfields we found experimental aircraft for long-range bombing, rockets designed to reach America, laboratories working on nuclear projects, stolen artworks, and vast caches of gold and currencies looted from all over Europe. We found factories hidden in mountains where they would be safe from air attack. We found huge rocket-launching sites too massive to destroy. And we found hordes of starved slave workers who manned all these facilities, and who were left to die when their strength ran out. The smell of death was overpowering as the corpses of laborers were simply left in piles to be removed when convenient.

The Germans I had encountered in our POW camps, especially those formerly engaged in intelligence activities, seemed particularly eager to engage our sympathies against the Russians. They sensed our antipathy to communism, and thought that in this cause they could emerge from their wartime wreckage as our natural ally. General Patton was sympathetic to this view, and consequently he staffed his military government with ex-Nazi officials even though this did not particularly please his superiors. While Military Governor of Bavaria, Patton was killed in a traffic accident. I remember him as a true leader who was the right one to have around when the going was tough. We all owed him a great debt of gratitude for his role in reversing the tide in our favor during the Battle of the Bulge, particularly at Bastogne.

◆ ◆ ◆

As the war on all fronts drew to a close, Bletchley Park became redundant insofar as Ultra intelligence was concerned. But the Enigma machine was a significantly helpful factor in the remodeling of my domestic life. As we moved through Germany, in mid-1945, we often came upon camps and installations that the retreating Germans had hastily evacuated. In one of these I found a working Enigma machine that the Germans had forgotten to take with them. General Bradley authorized me to take the machine back to Bletchley Park forthwith, using his own airplane and taking two weeks leave in Britain as a kind of reward. I took the latter seriously.

Through the Red Cross channel I got word to my erstwhile musical partner in London of my mission and suggested that in this peaceful interlude we might consider marriage, since it was highly uncertain if, when, or where we would ever meet again. To her British mind this seemed a reasonable enough proposition. After four years of war, one had to make the best of the conditions one faced, and this is what she did. There were no cautious inquiries about my family, or what life was like in Maplewood, New Jersey, or whether we lived in tree houses there. She and her family quickly organized a vicar, several neighbors and friends, and some carefully hoarded rations into a church wedding, a reception and feast. We were properly married and after a brief honeymoon, partly at the Savoy Hotel and partly in the idyllic surroundings of Ashdown Forest, back I flew to Germany.

It would be three months after I returned to the U.S. and demobilized before Decima could follow me. When she finally arrived, Maplewood welcomed her as its first war bride, and we immediately began to accept bookings as an Anglo-American musical entertainment duo of great charm and significance. It was interesting to note that she refused to adopt an American accent, American attitudes, or American ways of making tea. On July 4 the British flag was displayed at our home, along with the Stars and Stripes. The Queen's birthday was, and is, observed at our home, along with Guy Fawkes' Day and Boxing Day. But the first thing she did do on arriving here was to apply for U.S. citizenship.

12

Letters from Germany

WRITING TO MY mother and father from Germany presented an even greater challenge than from France or Luxembourg. Not only could I not write about my work, in addition we were not allowed to fraternize with the local Germans. No social gatherings, no dinners with the locals, no encounters with young lasses to write about. As a consequence, I had little option but to do a bit of bragging about what a good job I was doing even if I could not say what it was exactly. This not only helped fill the letters, but secretly I hoped it would convince them that I was a diligent and dutiful upholder of our family traditions. In fact, my new duties with the 9th Army under General Simpson had me embarking on an odyssey through *Mittel Europa*, with various pleasant as well as trying interludes that earned me a second Bronze Star:

> In the execution of plans for the effective exploitation of intelligence targets as Chief of the Targets Branch, G-2 Section, Headquarters Ninth U.S. Army, Major Button developed and placed into operation procedures for insuring the prompt dissemination of information concerning targets and for facilitating the operations of technical specialists in connection therewith. With outstanding intelligence and tireless energy he solved the varied and extensive problems that arose and contributed materially to the efficient collection of scientific knowledge for the United States and its Allies. The meritorious service of Major Button is in keeping with the high tradition of the military service.

♦ ♦ ♦

11 March 1945, Germany

MY FIRST GERMAN billet, which I just moved to, is a typical middle class home. The family had to leave in such a hurry that there was food in the kitchen just in the process of being prepared, and all the household belongings were just where they would normally be in the usual course of family life. There are the tools, the hammer, screwdriver, etc., on the cellar steps; the dust rags and carpet sweeper in the kitchen closet; the dishes, spotless, all in the cupboards, and the good glassware and cutlery in the sideboard. There were all the family clothes hanging in closets, and household linen neatly stacked in chests. Out back there is a small garden, a trash dump, two fat rabbits and a pile of coal. In the living room there was a daybed, a grandfather's clock and a piano. This is where I settled down, to sleep on the daybed, play the piano, and write on the table, read the excellent volume of Goethe I found here, and listen to the Germans trying to land shells in our section of town which they nowhere nearly do; they seem to think I am living about six miles in another direction!

For a minute or two I felt a little sad to see a home as completely and utterly brought to a halt this way. The people left so quickly the atmosphere had no time to leave with them, and the house seems to have caught itself in the middle of a gasp of astonishment. The people were apparently devout Catholics, judging from the crucifixes all around the house. They were also sentimental in the typical German manner—lots of framed mottoes to Heimat, Frauen and Kinder, etc. But two things dispelled any sentiment I had originally over the abrupt termination of their home life. One was the stack of Nazi flags in the attic, plus many party badges and pictures of Adolf—all tending to show that if they were good Catholics they were also good Party members, unless they did one or the other with tongue in cheek. I am sure one can't be honestly both. The other thing that relieved me of all concern for this family's well-being was the map on their kitchen wall. It was a map of the Ardennes offensive, with pins stuck in to show the line at the farthest extension, all the way to Marche in Belgium. Their hopes, apparently, remained pinned at Marche, for the map had never been changed after that. I thought back on those gloomy, frightening days and nights in Luxembourg. One of those Germans, running amuck in Belgium and Luxembourg exercising his heroism on the Ardennes peasants, came from this kitchen, and all the while his parents moved the little pins west and south, incidentally in my direction, feeling proud of their Hermann, wondering if 1940 were repeating itself. When I thought back on one night in particular, and now found myself in the very place the whole German offensive started from—a German home—I had a distinct impulse to burn the place down. However, it is a good billet and has a piano so I contented myself with liberating the two rabbits who are now happily eating up the spring greens in the garden. Besides, the Air Forces have already burned down most of the town. More news later. Thanks much for the coffee package. It was shared with some Dutch friends.

❖   ❖   ❖

28 March 1945

DEAR MISS HALE: [my piano teacher]

Once upon a time you used to draw word pictures for me to interpret the Rachmaninoff G Minor Prelude. They were very good pictures, prophetic ones, too, because what you described in large measure came true and followed the music perfectly. I experienced in reality everything the Prelude suggests, and now when I play it, I recall vividly the beautiful ancient city of Luxembourg during last December, when the war broke suddenly and furiously all around us, and then passed off in the distance, leaving us in that melancholy atmosphere of the Prelude's last few measures.

You know of course, the pace at which everyone moved across France. It was rapid, confident, and yet tragic in the destruction and vandalism that France itself had to undergo, the former by our bombs, the latter from the Germans. When the Allies reached Metz, Nancy, Luxembourg, eastern Belgium and Holland, the rush of the first two parts of the Prelude was over, and everything had to quiet down while the liberated countries tried to get untangled, the supplies brought to the lines and everything organized for the next effort. All that tumult and uproar of the second page, including the liberation of Paris and the excited welcome we received in so many French towns—all of this in a major key, quieted down. The music went back into minor, and an ominous sort of quiet descended and for a while we were left to our own devices while the Navy, the railroads and the air transport stacked up mountains of materiel in readiness for the final act.

During the lull I was in Luxembourg, which is an utterly charming city, completely medieval except for its trolley cars, which oddly enough are completely modern. And just as you used to say the soldier did, I lingered many times after duty with a very lovely Luxembourg girl, named Madeleine, who like all the Luxembourgers, hated the Germans with the last ounce of her energy, for they had robbed her youth of any of its normal pleasure and tried to make her generation think in ways they never would accept. The Americans brought back everything their lives had missed, and Madeleine, for one, blossomed like a flower in spring. We went to parties, had lots of music, made friends, learned new languages, and yet every now and then there was that reminder, underneath, that it was temporary, and that the war would call us back again any moment. And on the 16th of December we reached the point where that dreamy middle part of the music ends, with all that sense of reluctance to part, to be followed by an ominous rumbling, distant thunder, sudden gloom and terror spreading in the murky, fog-bound December air, until suddenly the uncertainty cleared, and the visible full-scale battle burst out like a long smothered fire. The frightening period was that in G minor, but when everything finally broke into the E-flat major passage, it was a battle between men, not ghosts, it was a time for trumpets, instead of stealth, and even the weather slid into major for the occasion. The issue was soon decided, as you know, but it was for that engagement only. Both sides rode away from the battlefield for another day, leaving a dismal scene of wreckage and ruined lives. The question, in the minds of all who saw it, was is there anywhere a Being or a Mind, which cares what men do to each other, or which has a Plan, of which this is all an essential part, or is it all as inevitable, as impersonal, as cold, dead and remote, as that single, final minor "G"?

Perhaps you see how prophetic your word-picture was, and why that piece means so much to me now.

My best love to Bertha and yourself.

❖ ❖ ❖

13 April 1945, Germany

[TRANSFERRED FROM 12th Army Group under Gen. Bradley to 9th Army HQ under Gen. Simpson]

There is considerably more to do that has direct contact with the war at Army than there was at Army Group. We move all over the place and see a great deal more of the mess than the Group people see. It was all most exciting on the night before the big Rhine crossing—with the unbelievable amount of artillery preparation and later all the planes and the complete German fold-up. Now everything is simply pell mell. Thousands of Germans trying to surrender. Thousands of French, Dutch and Belgians hiking along all roads leading back to their homes. Russians running wild all over the place with the Germans completely panic-stricken at the very sight of one of them. The Russian prisoners are killing every living German they can catch including cattle and horses and chickens, and the Germans came to our military government people for help against them. The best answer I have heard to a German was, "Well, who brought the Russians here?" The bombed towns in Germany are worse than any in England, although many factories remain intact. A banker in Dusseldorf told us that in spite of all the bombing, 80 percent of the city's industry remained in operation, the bombing simply destroying the residential sections. Most of the owners of factories are ready and eager to work for us, claiming they had never liked the Nazis anyway and had only joined under duress. This sort of thing makes us somewhat ill, or course. I flew around over Cologne a few weeks ago. The Germans were still just across the river, so we flew so low we could use the Cathedral towers for protection if any chose to pop at us. It is utter desolation, even the cemeteries were plowed up—the last "resting places" were anything but that. There are only frameworks of houses left. Everything is ashes and heaps of junk. But at Wesel there aren't even frameworks left. What at Cologne is wrecked, at Wesel is simply powder. You can tell there used to be a city there by the smell. There's not much else. The center of Munster is much like the center of Liverpool, and I felt a certain satisfaction in seeing how thoroughly the Germans had received their return payment. But nothing in England can compare with what has happened to these German cities.

The war, of course, is over. Only half an hour ago we heard that one of our armored divisions had crossed the Elbe River, and that is the last one before Berlin. If you don't hear from me for a while, I am either on the way home or en route to China. If the former, I will walk up Mountain Avenue. If the latter, I will be coming home via Millburn, so will take Wyoming Avenue instead.

◆ ◆ ◆

2 May 1945, Germany

I AM ABLE to report that once more, from being placed in a new position amongst new people, I have in three months been advanced to the position of head of a certain branch, with five officers and seven sergeants as a staff. The organization of this establishment to my liking has kept me exceedingly busy and while I haven't had time to write, I at least haven't had any time for mischief, facts which I present to counterbalance each other. In terms of billets, I have also progressed, having now a suite of two rooms, the living room having a Steinway grand, a sofa, a cabinet of fancy glassware and a large, full bookcase. The bedroom has two beds, a reading lamp, lace curtains and rugs. This front-line, foxhole existence as you can see is very rough and the hardships at the moment are immense. I forgot to add that the cellar is full of Rhine wine. My neighbor in this same house is one Don Linton, assistant V.P. of the New England Power Co. or is it New England Power & Light? On the other side of the fence, one of the corporals in the office is a J.C. Penney store layout man who used to earn $12,000 a year. He is forty-two years old. The local Provost Marshal is a state senator from North Carolina, while another colleague is the former Mayor of Cleveland.

The difference between being a staff body at Army Group, and being head of something at Army, is the same as between merely drawing pay, and actually going out and earning something. It is much more exciting all around. There's not much I can write in detail about. The atrocity stories you have been hearing are mostly true, I have seen a couple of them myself. On the other hand, spring in Germany is as beautiful as it is anywhere else.

❖   ❖   ❖

14 May 1945, Mittel Europa

I AM EXCEEDINGLY busy. I have a large branch now, and my "interests" run from the Rhine to Czechoslovakia and lots of other places. I have made many trips and among the most beautiful was the Harz Mountains and the vicinity of Gottingen; this part of the country in spring was wonderful. The officers I have in my branch are good sound workers, and seem to like their work which is all I ask; the men and particularly the sergeants are top-notch. They never grouse at having to work late, in fact sometimes they seem to want to work overtime when they get hold of a good idea. My administrative assistant is a lieutenant named Poole, who signs the memoranda he writes to me "Friday," and he is a veritable Friday in the assistance he renders. I am trying to get him a plane of his own so he can fly around and check things up for me; the job is much too extensive for automobiles.

Odd things happen. Yesterday, somebody walked into the office with several large boxes, and a receipt in his hand—he wanted some safe place to store the boxes. They were worth 130 million marks and contained the scepter, crown, cross and two swords of Charlemagne. I believe they were replicas containing the jewels from the originals. Charlemagne wore about a seven and a half size hat. The scabbards of the swords were all full of pearls, rubies, diamonds, gold, etc, etc, etc. I was reluctant to sign the receipt, and turned it over to the military police for safeguarding. (Ten marks = one dollar).

A little German boy declared to me that the American bombers were good, and operated only on factories, etc., but he thought others were cowards for bombing at night.

The land is full of carpetbaggers disguised as scientific experts, technicians "studying" German and a lot of people with phony research jobs, all duplicating each other and ferreting out the stores of wine and schnapps.

I have an unbelievably "rich" Steinway grand. Thank goodness. It can be made to sound like an entire symphony orchestra, and has a quality of precision and delicacy in the high notes that often rich-toned pianos lack. I have a lot of fun on it, and in this land of "non-fraternization" it is a very satisfying companion.

I have seen all the V-1 bombs and V-2 rockets in their underground factories and it is interesting to study them for a change instead of jumping ten feet out of bed when one lands nearby or goes thudding by overhead. You go along thru this beautiful countryside and suddenly you see a cave, and there will be a complete store of the most utterly lethal objects; it is the *Niebelung's* hoard and it is becoming apparent that the legend is more true than what we were led to believe was "reality."

Still the Germans do everything better than other Europeans. They clean house better than Poles, Russians, French or others, so we have German maids. They set about cleaning up their wrecked villages while the French would stand on a corner for days and argue about the number of hours a day they could work to repair damage. The German girls all look like a combination of Libby Earl and Betsy Dunlap, and have good posture and proper walk, while the French—well, why elaborate. Against all this the sight of one concentration camp destroys the whole build-up.

Summer is fully upon us and I am feeling a little lazy—there's no lawn mower in the house, otherwise I would cut the grass just to keep in practice. I have a willow tree, lots of tulips and iris and those white flowers that grow on a certain kind of hedge, and four lilac bushes and some lilies of the valley, so all in all its quite fragrant.

❖ ❖ ❖

15 May 1945, Braunschweig

THE PRESENT CIRCUMSTANCES keep me so busy I am overlooking all sorts of things to wit your wedding anniversary. But you would be very satisfied if I could tell you of all the details of my job, and how it is being done to the thorough approval of my bosses. The G-2 executive officer just spent a good half hour here asking me all sorts of questions about my branch, inquiring as to along what lines he could assist me on the higher level, and saying that he was "exceedingly pleased with the way I was handling this job." This is all the more music to my ears, because when I first came to 9th Army, the head man would not let me be put into the branch chief's job because I was a "very young" major, relatively. Now I have proved that there is a darn good reason for my being a major and the boss is apparently convinced too.

In addition to my office, I have three airplanes, a Mercedes Benz and several other less auspicious cars to use, a private radio net lent me by the Navy and all sorts of other tricks and devices. I have to do business with all kinds of people, British mostly after Americans, but two Chinese majors came in today and we had a field day bowing and exclaiming what an honor it was—they were honored, we were honored, China was honored, U.S. was honored, 9th Army was honored, etc., etc. You will ask what in the world is it all about? I can only say it is interesting and absorbing.

All day long yesterday we had the Russians here. Everybody stared and stared—it being a little hard to converse. The Germans in Braunschweig (Brunswick) having seen the Russians here, are now in an utter panic for fear we will turn the place over to the Reds! Everyone got roaring drunk, but my observation was that the Russians held theirs very well. They were a rough looking lot. And they had some of their girl soldiers with them, with physiques that were nothing if not robust.

In this job I think if it were private industry I would be equal to a general manager–V.P. at about $8,000. Alas.

◆   ◆   ◆

18 May 1945, Braunschweig

JUST RETURNED FROM a trip. I left Brunswick after lunch, stopped for some business at Kassel and went on to Bad Nauheim, where I spent the night. The pilot got somewhat bored on such a long flight, so he turned the plane over to me and I flew it for an hour. It doesn't go very fast and practically steers itself, so we were fairly safe. It was a beautiful day, and all of Germany spread out beneath us in many colors and shades. Bad Nauheim is a famous resort, complete with hotels a la Saratoga Springs, with mineral baths, lush vegetation and a fairly cosmopolitan population. The hotel for visiting officers was the best in town and boasted the best Steinway I have played yet, which is saying something. Breakfast was fruit cup, cereal, two eggs, sausage and toast and coffee, after which we took off for Wiesbaden. The latter has been somewhat bombed, but is rapidly coming back to life, as is the rest of Germany. Lunch in Wiesbaden, after which we flew back to Kassel, then to Brunswick.

I receive touching letters from our English cousins and friends on the subject of Roosevelt's death.

❖   ❖   ❖

28 May 1945, Brunswick

THE OTHER DAY I drove down to Magdeburg, on the Elbe, to have a look at Asia. Asia is the other side of the Elbe, where the Russians' area begins, and the Magdeburg Germans look in that direction with the most obvious fear and trembling. The main bridge across the river is one of the old structures with ancient stone towers at each end. However the towers at the Russian end were demolished, and the bridge is down in the middle, which leaves two towers on the west side standing like a last outpost of Europe before Asia begins. I call it Asia because that was the description given it by Paul Sapieha, my Polish friend, who made several visits to the other side in the capacity of interpreter. Paul's ancestors have fought Russians for centuries. When he, upon returning, sort of shuddered and said "It's Asia over there," he spoke the feeling of all the Europeans who have feared Asia since the Dark Ages. It was centuries of meaning in one sentence.

I was with an English Colonel. We walked over the pontoon bridge to the Russian side, where there was a very Mongolian-looking sentry with a tommy gun. Down came a Russian major and a captain to greet us. One doesn't go any further than the edge of the river. The two officers were good, neat-looking soldiers, and could speak German so we had a bull session with them. The major was thirty, came from Ostrov and had fought for three years without a leave. The captain came from Odessa, which he said was a worse ruin than Magdeburg. He was a very pleasant, well-spoken, civilized person, with four decorations for gallantry. We debated very ordinary topics like how did you get to be a captain, and how the food was, and what were the towns like in Russia, but each person was most careful to avoid any really searching questions. I tried one and the major blandly pretended he didn't understand my German, which was a good "out." We took pictures all around and saluted several times and shook hands, and they returned to Asia, we to Europe.

Lined up on the Asiatic side was a column of French and Belgian refugees returning to their countries. At a given signal the column moved on to the bridge and slowly across it, pushing all kinds of carts and carriages, in all manner of clothes, all looking beaten but everyone as he or she reached the U.S. sentry on the west side seemed to straighten up, smile and try to wave or salute. Many broke out French and Belgian flags, sticking them on the tops of their carts, and you could see the pride they took in that, in spite of their wretched condition. Then a line of trucks, General Motors' best driven by Soviet soldiers, came across filled with more refugees, also bravely waving their flags, some with pathetic but carefully made attempts at a U.S. flag sewn together with bits of old rags and odds and ends of nearly everything. We waved at each truck, and the response was practically hysterical. I tried a "*Vive la France*" once at a truckload of Frenchmen and they hollered and roared with delight until they were out of sight. The Russian guards had a very good way of spotting people they suspected were not refugees but possibly Germans trying to escape; they simply stopped any male who wasn't carrying anything. He would either be a German soldier or some other unsavory character. Many of the women were wheeling baby carriages full of babies; I guess women will have babies no matter what the circumstances.

The town of Magdeburg was a burnt-out shell, but plenty of civilians were there and everybody was shoveling, sweeping and building, as if determined to make their town a buttress against Asia, across the river.

We had a most beautiful songfest at a hotel in Goslar the other night. Goslar is a resort right at the foot of the Harz Mountains, a perfect setting. The hotel is run by U.S. troops, but has a corny orchestra of Italian ex-prisoner laborers; you can tell they never wanted to be Romans or conquerors, they just want to sit happily squeezing out "O Sole Mio" on the accordion and this they did for hours on end, till we sent them to bed and I took over the piano with one Evelyn Ames of NBC (singer) and many other friends and we sang till 4:30 AM.

❖ ❖ ❖

15 June 1945, Brunswick

YOU MUST CALL Bill Winslow and tell him I just spent the day with a party that included Larry Riedel, V.P. of General Motors, and a good friend of Bill's. Others in the party were the President of Chrysler Export, Vice-Presidents of Proctor & Gamble, Ford, and Yale & Towne, plus a major general and a few colonels. We went around to a few important German industrial and scientific establishments that I have a certain degree of responsibility for. The party was a committee sent over here to study certain armament-related subjects and also to "see for themselves" what was doing in Germany. I hope their eyes were opened to the fact that although we may have lots of everything in America, it isn't always the most advanced. In some tricks the Germans were fifty to a hundred years ahead of us. This is because war is their business, and is not ours. I will tell you more about this later.

In a nearby town a couple of Hitler youths were caught the other night trying to lay some mines in a road. So the Military Governor of the place put out a proclamation that if there were any more such pranks, every house in Goslar would have a Russian billeted in it. Nothing more has happened.

✦ ✦ ✦

25 June 1945

It's HARD TO tell where to start. A short while ago I packed everything into a Mercedes just as I used to pack up the Ford, and set off from Brunswick on a southerly course which took me thru the Harz Mts. to Nordhausen. Nordhausen is where the Germans had built a mass-production V-1 and V-2 factory completely inside a mountain. Having been on the receiving end of both weapons, I now stood in the evil-looking pit from which these weird devices erupted, just like some kind of spiteful gesture from hell itself. As a matter of fact, Milton would have found that analogy perfect, for a V-2 rocket going up looks like something Satan might have tried to hurl at heaven. The factory was supposed to produce nine hundred a month (V-2) and about four times as many V-1's. Nine hundred is an amazing figure when you know how big a rocket is, and how complicated. There are rows of partly finished ones standing inside the mountain like giants, and they have a living quality about them that gives the whole place the atmosphere of a nightmare. More so when you realize that it was a slave-labor place, with miserable wretches from all Europe forced to live and work until they died inside the mountain. If they dropped at work, for exhaustion or illness, the SS guards whipped them till they died, when they were taken out and cremated just at the entrance of the tunnel. There was never, in Milton's or Dante's furthest imagination, any such colossal evil or complete fulfillment of the "Seventh Circle of Hades" as Nordhausen. And had the invasion come six months later, or had the Ardennes battle tipped just slightly the other way, the output of that mountain would have completely destroyed London, there is no question of that fact at all. Furthermore we found plans for advanced versions of V-2 that could easily carry all the way to America, not just the coast, but well inland to say Detroit. They do this by a wing arrangement that permits the rocket to glide from the stratosphere to almost anywhere desired. This is a fact that our country should know. I am not sure the papers are permitted to say anything about it but they should be.

Well, I went from there to Weimar and ended up at Jena where Carl Zeiss makes such terrific cameras, but not being a camera fan particularly I made no attempt to get the most valuable type. I thought of going on to Czechoslovakia but it was getting late. So I stayed overnight in a little town called Possneck and the next day set forth for points west. We are not supposed to fool around too close to the Russians.

I drove thru middle Germany to Gotha, Eisenach, marvelous medieval towns—and then off thru byways to Wiesbaden on the Rhine. Here I took a room with my old friends, Gen. Sibert & Company. Things being in a state of confusion, generally, I set forth again, this time with a driver, a good boy from Montana who can prepare fish and shoot game. We headed for the Alps, and spent the first night in Augsburg. The next day we went to Munich, where I visited all the places where Anne Sisson and I used to bicycle and eat ice-cream. Most of them were rubble and ash. From Munich we went straight to Berchtesgaden and at 5:30 PM, in a magnificent many-colored sunset, I reached the end of the trail from Maplewood to Hitler's mountaintop. It is useless to try to describe the beauty of the place itself, with snow covered peaks on all sides and Berchtesgaden way down below and the green country of Bavaria off to the northward. Hitler, Goering, Bormann, etc. had homes halfway up the mountains, while Eagle's Nest itself is a stone house right on top, from which you can see the whole world. There are two conference rooms in it, a kitchen and a few small rooms. There they held meetings. There Adolf thought and, by some distortion of Nature's meaning, turned the grandeur of the scene into all the perverse and foolish notions that landed him in the underground incinerator of Berlin. The homes themselves, halfway up the mountain, were directly hit by the Air Force and destroyed.

I stayed in the Berchtesgaden Hof making note that I should return thither at the earliest opportunity. Each room has a balcony, with chair and table, and the view is there for whatever use one makes of it. You know Alpine scenery, so I won't try to tell you what this was like. The Konigsee, about a mile and a half away, reflects everything around it and is alternately mirror and diamond, depending on the angle of the sun.

The next day we drove to Innsbruck, thru all sorts of Alps. From Innsbruck one has to go to Italy if possible, and again at sunset. I found myself at Brenner Pass, where Adolf and Benito used to meet. This is a small town in a valley between gigantic peaks, most of which still had snow. We set forth into Italy and then withdrew into Austria. Nearby was a small lake with a weather platoon living on the shore in a farmhouse. We dropped in there and found a Lt. and a Capt. about to go fishing. We joined them and spent the evening in the boat and around the shores, catching in all five fish. The full moon came out from behind a peak at about nine, and it was absolutely and perfectly beautiful. At ten we took our fish into the farmhouse, cleaned and fried them and up until midnight had the most delicious fish and red wine party I have ever enjoyed. Slept till nine and then took off for Innsbruck. From there we drove up to the German border to a town called Fussen. This was interesting to me, because in 1934 I rode my bicycle to Fussen from the north, and had to stop at the border because of the Austrian revolution then in progress. So now I could drive up to Fussen from the south and see what I had been denied then. Like going behind the Looking Glass.

We cruised from there back towards Wiesbaden over some of the same roads I had bicycled over in 1934, stopping here and there for a beer, cooking lunch over a fire by another small lake, where we had a quick dip and finally arriving back in Wiesbaden at evening. Here I find the general wants me to go to London, so I'm off again tomorrow or the next day, in a plane this time.

6 July 1945

WHAT HAPPENED WAS this: I had seven days leave to go to London, so I took off from Wiesbaden and arrived here on Thursday. Decima and I agreed that it was now or never, so we'd better get on with it. The relatives (etc.) could not be collected and details of the wedding arranged before Sunday or Monday, and as people can't get married on Sunday we settled for 2 o'clock Monday afternoon. My best man was Stuart Edwards, an English officer with whom I used to work. Outside of Stuart, I was represented by Vi and Mrs. Niggeman, Lady Leith Ross and a Canadian officer who will shortly phone you to say he was there. His name is Pat Murphy. Decima wore white and carried some fragrant sort of vegetation but I don't know the details of her apparel and will leave that to the bride.

We went to an Olde English Country Inn in a forest in Sussex for three days and now are back at the hotel hoping my plane won't be able to take off tomorrow.

Thank you for your wire and John and Grace's too. I felt fairly miserable not having you there and having to pack into such a short time what could have been a wonderful party if we had had time to organize it. Even as it was it was a good affair. The pictures are good and we will send you all of them.

I believe my wife is already having a good effect on me and I think you will like her. She has more get up and go than I have. We have a piano in our suite here and are having lots of fun with it, both in long-hair and short. She can sing all types.

I go back now to Germany and she goes on with her current show. That keeps her pretty busy. But in spite of that she is an exceedingly wifely type of girl and I think I have struck a good thing.

❖   ❖   ❖

Summer 1945, Goslar, Germany

ABOUT GERMANY, THEN. The English will need no warning, and the Americans will heed none. But Germany is not destroyed, nor even totally subdued, and unless watched at every turn, will not only be ready to make another war in an astonishingly short time, but will do so with weapons that make fleets of four-engined bombers as antique as the steam automobile. I won't burden you with descriptions of bombed cities, except to say that they are worse than any English cities that had been bombed. I have been studying what was un-bombed, and what is underground, and what kind of things they were experimenting on. First, the I.G. Farben Industries, Germany's biggest chemical trust, maybe the world's biggest, although constituting some of the prime bombing target material in Germany and busily engaged in making all sorts of things, was practically un-bombed throughout the war, and today goes merrily on its way, giving rise to all kinds of darksome speculation amongst staffs. Then, what the Germans have underground is simply a fulfillment of the legend of the *Niebelungen*. They have two Germanys: one beautifully landscaped with forests and green fields and buxom farm lassies, and another underground, teeming with miserable slaves, making the huge shiny evilly beautiful V-2s and V-1s, laboratories with almost Hollywood-style arrays of test tubes, microscopes, wind tunnels, chemicals, and stores of explosives, complete cities inside of mountains, and deep in salt mines, stores of archives, museum records dating back to 800 A.D., all stowed away as far down as twelve hundred meters into the earth. This is why I think that Germany is more dangerous than ever; all the bombing in the world would not have stopped the V-2 factories, and throughout Germany, the smallest back-yard factory could make parts for these things. The day of huge cannon is long past already. And the devices to destroy bombers were so near to perfection that one doesn't like to picture what might have occurred.

The people are trying to make friends now. I think the scientists want to help get things going again, some because of fear of the Russians, some to get back at us some time in the future. My housemaid takes the greatest care to have fresh flowers in the room every day. The local stands are most careful to provide us with their best produce. Many people stop us to curse and rail loudly at Hitler. But there are still occasional wires stretched across roads, and petty attempts to create annoyances. When something untoward occurs in a town, a couple of houses are burned down and nothing happens after that.

◆ ◆ ◆

2 September 1945, Frankfurt

BOB SHACKLETON has returned and given an account of how he got in touch with you. I had dinner with him last night at his place, Bad Nauheim, which is about twenty miles north of here. General Eisenhower's secretary, Kay Summersby by name (English), was going up there too so she arranged to get the General's car for us to go in. Only it turned out that the General himself was also going to Bad Nauheim, and as he didn't see the sense of two cars going there, we all went together, Kay and I and General Ike. He was in good form. It seems he has just disposed of a group of visiting congressmen by telling them frankly that in the new atomic bomb era, they knew as much about war as he did. I asked him what would be taught at West Point now in the way of tactics, but he couldn't imagine. He had recently returned from Belfast, where they had given him the freedom of the city. Some Irish dignitary got up and delivered such a terrific tribute that Ike said, "After a few minutes I thought he was talking about three other guys!" Ike is very talkative, and completely natural.

We arrived at Bad Nauheim to find a group consisting of two American girls, Bob S., his colleague Henry Lee Munson of N.Y.C.

who is also a major, and a rather aesthetic captain who turned out to be Tommy Phipps (not the Englewood crowd, the Vanderbilt side) who works in the Public Relations Bureau somewhere here. He likes to sing too, so as the evening wore on Shackleton and Phipps developed into a real bowler-hat 1890 corny vaudeville team. We had a lot of fun. Munson and Kay covered all the court gossip while this was going on, and I caught up on that en route back to Frankfurt with Kay.

We got back at two, had a sandwich in the snack bar, and so to bed. I could not help thinking that Decima would have been so much of an addition to such a party, both because of music and because she has the faculty of listening to a different conversation with each ear, and thus would be able to tell me all I had missed. On the other hand, she wouldn't enter into such talk too readily, for she is completely natural, and depends on herself, whereas company like this sometimes is a little stilted and unnatural, with people depending on others for gossip, tips and advancement. Except for General Ike, whose utter naturalness so completely won the English who, one suspects at times, are beginning to be a little tired of their own stuffiness as a nation. Ike, incidentally, got a bigger turnout in Belfast than even the King and Queen, which may indicate something.

Did I tell you that Carroll Gibbons, who plays the piano and runs the orchestra at the Savoy in London (best hotel in town) offered me his job while he went on a ten-week vacation? I couldn't take it, but would have liked to!

◆ ◆ ◆

This ends my wartime correspondence to my parents, "M. and P."

The author and his bride, Decima Knight, are flanked on the right by Leslie Henson, a leading theatrical performer, and on the left by best man, British Captain Stuart Edwards, a close associate from Bletchley Park.

Three members of "The Leslie Henson Gaieties"—Henson, Decima Knight, and Tommy Trinder—in Algiers, 1941, at the first broadcast of the Armed Forces radio network in North Africa.

The author with U.S. Army code experts intercepting lower level German radio field code and plotting the appropriate military intervention. Field code could be decrypted on the spot, whereas that from German Enigma cipher machines was processed at Bletchley Park.

Louis Armstrong was one of the many entertainers who volunteered their talents to Voice of America for broadcasting and telecasting to countries around the globe. Some of his biggest fans were in countries behind the Iron Curtain. (USIA photo)

President Dwight D. Eisenhower, escorted by the author, on a visit to the Voice of America broadcasting control room in Washington D.C. The newscaster at the microphone could have been speaking in any one of the 45 languages used at VOA. (USIA photo)

The author and his family at their home in Paris, during the time he was in the diplomatic corps assigned to NATO.

The Bob Button Orchestra entertains young and old alike who love music of the 1930's and 1940's. They perform at town events, local clubs, and service organizations.

The musical alliance of Decima and Bob Button that began in England during wartime continues to entertain audiences today in Connecticut.

13

Life after Enigma

As THE EUROPEAN Theater of War came to an end, so did the interception and reading of German wireless communications. But history teaches that this activity never really slows up; it is only necessary to find new targets to penetrate. At the end of the war, the British, with their usual political insight, mounted an expedition to Berlin to seize a warehouse where the Germans had stored all the Enigma machines. The plan was to sell or otherwise distribute these machines to countries anywhere in the world. As long as the Ultra secret remained secret—that the British could decrypt Enigma code—those at Bletchley Park would continue to read anybody's mail they chose to, friend or potential foe. The official thirty-year blackout on revealing that fact was quite enough to preserve the postwar balance of power. Russia became the prime target, of course, but who could say what plots were being hatched in Uruguay or Ceylon? One could always listen in and forestall them. Thus the code-breakers were kept busy, and are to this day, aided by a steady stream of new technology.

To many demobilized GI's, especially those who, like myself, were draftees, the end of the war meant a return to a home environment, a familiar job, and involvement in community affairs. I had all of these on my mind, but they were now influenced by a worldview, which had been opened to me by the Enigma experience with all of its military, political, scientific, diplomatic, and historical aspects. As it turned out, the whole of my post-war career involved all of these areas.

Initially I returned to my former employer, NBC, as a sales account executive. As such, I had just enough influence on broadcasting program content to be able to cajole top management into carrying the historic Iron Curtain speech by Sir Winston Churchill at Fulton, Missouri, that marked the beginning of the Cold War. Next, an invitation from the Pentagon involved me in this cold war from a military point of view, obliquely referred to as "psychological warfare." This, in turn, led to becoming director of the worldwide broadcasting arm of the government, the Voice of America, which, in spite of its peaceful facade, contributed mightily to the eventual collapse of the Berlin Wall and the break-up of the Soviet empire. After a NATO posting, I joined Communications Satellite Corporation where my role called into play all previous diplomatic, political, military experiences. Working with the new technology of satellite communications made national boundaries obsolete and interception of global communications commonplace. More details will follow, along with the domestic and musical accompaniment that brought all these roles into mutual harmony. But first, back to NBC.

Life at NBC had taken on the new challenge of television, which had to establish itself as a medium of entertainment and public service, news and education, and most important of all, commercial advertising. I had the good fortune of being in on the early days of these activities. For several years, between 1946 and 1954, I lost interest in international intrigues and devoted all my attention to helping the development of this new medium. As one of a new breed, a TV advertising salesman, I cornered the first commercials for two landmark TV stars—Dave Garroway with his "Today" show and Ralph Edwards with his "This Is Your Life." I believe both shows are probably still running in syndication somewhere in the world.

There was a lively war already going on in my civilian occupation, a war between NBC and CBS, between Bill Paley and David Sarnoff of RCA, parent of NBC. This was a battle for audience in which each network raided the other and made off with star talent, programs, and rich sponsors. Money, of course, was the ammunition. The troops were known as hucksters. The spoils of this war were the big-name stars like

Jack Benny, Bob Hope, Fred Allen, Ozzie and Harriet Nelson, Dave Garroway, Fibber McGee and Mollie, Ralph Edwards, and others. In this war, I served in the front lines, with positions at the 21 Club, Toots Shor, and the English Grill at Rockefeller Plaza. The weapons were martinis, manhattans, and expense accounts. It was the Battle of Madison Avenue, with each side wearing the same uniform—pin stripe suits and sincere ties. It was a great time to be alive.

It was also a precarious time. There was a different kind of war brewing in the world, a cold war with Russian communism stirring up insurrection here at home and around the world. Between martinis at the English Grill, I would occasionally pause to reflect on what options I might have should the Cold War heat up and my status as a reserve officer in Secret Intelligence come to the attention of somebody in Washington. I was not long left in doubt. That is exactly what happened.

A letter came to the president of NBC from the Deputy Secretary of Defense inquiring as to whether I might be granted a year's leave of absence from NBC to assist with certain activities at the Pentagon for which my past experience and abilities made me eminently suitable. The NBC president was Pat Weaver, a Dartmouth graduate. He saw some advantage in cooperating with an obviously high level activity of the government, so permission was granted for my leave of absence, not for military duty, but for a shadowy entity in the Pentagon called the Office of Special Operations (OSO). This type of office usually handles assignments that are unattributable or that the head office does not wish to acknowledge ever happened at all.

In fact, the name of the office was all that anybody knew about it, except for the people in it—about eight or ten, including secretaries. The staff wore no service uniforms, although they were of the Army, Navy, Air Force, Marines, and the CIA. Everything about the place and the people was highly classified. Nobody said anything, nobody did anything, it seemed, yet the phones were always busy, the secretaries were always typing, and the conference room was always occupied with meetings. I never saw anybody arrive or depart from the meetings. They materialized and vanished, like the CIA colonel in the popular sitcom of the eighties, "MASH."

The office occupied a unique niche in the hierarchy of the Pentagon. It reported to, or was under, the Deputy Secretary of Defense. This meant that the Secretary of Defense could always deny its existence, or say he did not know what it was up to. This is what deputy anythings are for. They do things that the boss wants done but does not want any responsibility for. Thus the State Department has a secretary, but he is usually out making speeches in Upper Volta, while the ordinary business of the department is being conducted by the undersecretary, who has a deputy who does the real business, which involves matters about which the secretary would rather not be informed, but which he hopes get done.

Something about my work in the OSO office reminded me of my earlier days at NBC as the "Mysterious Mr. Button." I mixed with the Secretary of Defense and other chiefs and worked with high-level intelligence operatives and covert associates, but I cannot write about my duties other than to say it drew on my wartime experience. For all I know the work is still classified. Fortunately, no one ever asked me what I did there, except my daughters. And I could not tell them either.

Toward the end of my year's leave of absence from NBC, during which I was occupied with sundry classified projects, I received a message from the U.S. Information Agency, parent organization of the Voice of America (VOA). Senator Joseph McCarthy had just attacked VOA for what he thought was a propaganda position, "soft on communism." His scurrilous tactics and character innuendo had devastated staff morale at VOA, and the current management was both incompetent and naive in the political cesspool that McCarthy had created in Washington. The remedy seemed to lie in a change, replacing the current director with someone nonpolitical, broadcast-oriented, with added assets such as military and intelligence experience as a kind of endorsement or insurance of a right attitude against both McCarthyism and communism. This prospect suited my taste and capabilities and appealed to me more than did life at the English Grill or Madison Avenue. I asked NBC for an extension of my leave of absence. This granted, I presently became the new Director of Voice of America, the U.S. overseas broadcasting service, with a worldwide staff of about two thousand employees and an annual budget of about 24 million dollars.

The Voice of America was just beginning television operations to meet the rapid development of this medium abroad, and within three years VOA would be telecasting to more than 150 television stations in the Free World. Its established radio broadcasting programs were sent on short wave in forty-five languages worldwide, including to the Iron Curtain countries. In addition, there was a global English language service. The substance of the programs was a mix of news, current events, entertainment, and U.S. foreign policy. For news we had the usual sources such as AP, UPI, and INS. But for news of events within countries under dictatorships with a fully controlled press, we had to rely on secret agents to send out accounts of what was really going on there. Our acknowledgment of receipt of such information took the form of including in our broadcast programs a particular piece of classical music. Beethoven's Fifth Symphony was our agents' favorite, but it was also preferred by our opponents as well, so we had to interpret the music both ways. I wrote about the VOA in an anecdotal story for *Greenwich Time*.

◆ ◆ ◆

When I became Director of the Voice of America, everyone in Washington had a different idea of what the Voice was doing, or was supposed to be doing.

President Eisenhower thought the nation should have a big public relations agency to include the Voice and other media that would explain our policies (if anyone could say what they were) to a world-wide audience.

The State Department under John Foster Dulles thought that the Voice should speak with a loud sound, but not say anything of significance.

The Pentagon thought that the Voice should put out a constant drum roll of anti-soviet propaganda. If we didn't, they said, they would hire General Sarnoff and do it themselves.

Senator Joe McCarthy thought, and publicly protested, that the Voice was under the covert control of crypto-Communists whom he would expose. He never did, because there weren't any.

The CIA used the Voice in various ways but would never admit it. The Voice occasionally used the CIA too, but also would never admit it.

Junketing Congressmen used overseas posts of the Voice in ways nobody will ever tell, but this was a two-way street because these same dignitaries at various times had to vote yea or nay on the Voice's budget.

David Sarnoff, the biggest person in the business world of communications, wanted the Voice to run commercials for freedom and democracy and peace. He wanted slogans, similar in tone to "LSMFT—Lucky Strike Means Fine Tobacco." The State Department, aghast, sent me warnings against showing any such obvious enthusiasm.

NBC, CBS, and ABC were constantly on guard lest anybody in the USA should hear Voice broadcasts. This was their job, they insisted. Voice of America was for other peoples, not Americans, even though Americans paid for it and ran it and made speeches about it at Rotary Clubs and ladies luncheons all across the land.

Finally, there were forty-five different language desks in the organization, with at least that many different views on how to explain American ways and policies to their target audiences. Not very far beneath the surface simmered all the differences of race, histories and religious beliefs represented among all these nationalities. Translation alone posed a major problem. We couldn't find an American who was fluent in Uzbek, for example; we had to use a German. Consider the potential opportunities for subtlety in translation from State Department diplomatic into English, then into

German to emerge as a commentary in Uzbek. As VOA Director I had to take responsibility for the result. It was excellent training for dealing with Congressional inquiries and debate. Do Uzbeks vote, I was once asked by an incredulous Congressman.

I had a total staff of about two hundred. Politically speaking they could be divided up as liberal, conservative and Iranian, meaning that I could generally understand the first two but never the third. As we all know, they haven't changed. My desk calendar in those days reveals more arbitration of disputes originating among the Iranian staff than in any other language service.

Given all these cross-currents and tension-raising relationships, I had recourse to a remedy for which I was well equipped. As is generally known, I am often guilty of playing the piano in public when I perhaps should be doing something more serious or boring. The one common denominator amongst all the various Voice nationalities was a love of music and indeed an ability to perform it. In no time at all it became apparent that our safety valve should take the form of a multinational revue, complete with chorus line, small orchestra, soloists, and all the trappings of Broadway, NY, the Ginza of Tokyo, the Reeperbahn of Hamburg, the Casbahs of North Africa and everywhere in between. The talent came out from behind desks, studios, closets. We found that shapely legs had little to do with nationality. The popular music of every land began to be blended into a musical extravaganza that could not have been duplicated anywhere else in the world, except perhaps in the BBC International Service, but probably not even there because the British do not normally act this way.

There were skits poking fun at officialdom, original songs in every tongue, a pleasant artistic rivalry and, both in rehearsal and after performances, a new spirit of friendliness and cooperation. The Voice of America had become a fun place, instead of a whipping dog for the likes of Sen. McCarthy. All the émigrés, the new U.S. citizens, the expatriates for whatever reason, found out that laughter and music are ways to rise above tension and political torpor. Respect for democracy thrived, along with a healthy irreverence for pompous politicians.

So whatever else I accomplished for the Cold War while I directed our overseas broadcasts, I always felt that I had opened the doors a bit and let light and sound into what had been a closed-in system. Music was the therapy, and the release of tension it brought in turn released new talent in all our people, which in turn just may have given the Voice of America that added vitality that made its programs an essential ingredient in the lives of people around the world.

◆ ◆ ◆

Explanation of U.S. foreign policy was the province of the State Department, which generally had the attitude that the less the public knew the better. President Eisenhower took the opposite point of view. He was public relations oriented and believed that truth, sometimes unvarnished, was the best propaganda. The VOA, started in 1946, proved to be an effective counter-propaganda effort against the trash of Dr. Goebbels, Stalin, and Tokyo Rose. One day, President Eisenhower came to visit the VOA on Independence Avenue. It was my privilege to show him around. I took him through the control room studios and offices and introduced him to some of our more glamorous newscasters and commentators. He scratched his ear in disbelief. "I had no idea," he said, "that we were doing all this." From then on, he took a personal interest in what the VOA was telling the world. For example, in 1956, when the Russians were trying to subdue the Hungarians, Ike—well aware of our efforts to encourage anti-Russian sentiment but also of the risks involved—came to our offices personally to warn us not to let the Hungarians think that the U.S. 7th Army in Germany was about to come to their rescue. This would start World War III, he knew, and he did not want that. Besides, our principal allies, Britain and France, were so preoccupied with Egypt and the Suez Canal that they had no spare time for Hungary. And Ike liked to have allies, particularly the British.

My administrative duties at the VOA included handling the personnel problems of all forty-five foreign nationalities on the staff, including our Americans. In the course of these events, I picked up a few phrases of Russian, Mandarin, Persian, and Korean that I used on occasion to lend authenticity to my remarks when testifying before Congress on the subject of our budget. Nothing influenced Senator Lyndon Johnson, when interrogating me, as much as a reply containing a phrase or two in Uzbek. Johnson treated it all as a game. If I one-upped him, I got a budget approval. If he one-upped me, he got a headline in the *Washington Post*. It was all great fun. Gradually the dark shadow of Joseph McCarthy melted away. The Voice of America became a happy team of coworkers. We even gained some compliments from our chief competitors in international broadcasting, the venerable BBC.

Another duty of a director is to inspect everything. When this involves bases around the world, the travel schedule can become formidable. The VOA had transmitter sites in the UK, Germany, Finland, the island of Rhodes, Eritrea, the Philippines, and Australia, plus working arrangements with certain indigenous posts like Bangkok and Beirut. In Bangkok I met the King, who was an expert on the xylophone. My most pleasant duty there was to accompany him on the piano. At one point he called in his ten-piece Police Department band to play with us, and not a single royal discord was heard. The King and I were right in tune.

Many felt the Voice of America's greatest achievement was its contribution to the gradual crumbling of the Communist monolith of Eastern Europe, controlled by the Soviet Union. We knew, through agents and defectors from Iron Curtain countries, that VOA broadcasts were keeping alive the hope for freedom. Many risked their lives to send clandestine messages into our various language services, encouraging and informing our broadcasters of conditions in their country. We knew we had a large audience out there, which, like a steam kettle, was likely to pop at the right opportunity. One of our star entertainers, disk jockey Willis Conover, was as well known and liked in the Iron Curtain countries as Stalin was the opposite.

Russian attempts to jam our broadcasts were operated with military precision. Whenever they did so, we, with equal agility, switched frequencies. It was like an electronic game, albeit a deadly one, for the line between war and peace in electronics is a shadowy one. In this case, both sides were rehearsing for the real thing. But the Cold War never, in my time, became "hot." I believe the psychological and intellectual propagandistic tactics pursued by the free world through such means as the Voice of America and its covert relative Radio Free Europe were more effective than any explosives. We found we had more friends than we ever realized, and live friends are better than dead enemies.

While the VOA was the experience of a lifetime, my leave of absence from NBC, from Toots Shorr and Madison Avenue, was growing thin. The government, in the form of the Civil Service, wondered what my status was. So did NBC. And so did I. It was suggested that if I chose to remain with the government, a tour of duty in the Foreign Service was a career requisite, and I was offered my choice of several assignments.

NBC offered me my job back as a senior account executive with unlimited access to Toots Shor, the English Grill at Rockefeller Plaza, and even the 21 Club, all in the interest of client relations. After all, I had provided the first sponsor for "This Is Your Life"—Hazel Bishop No-Smear Lipstick. This sponsorship kept the show financially alive until it suddenly caught on everywhere, in spite of its dubious relevance to lipstick. Also, I had secured the first sponsor for the first morning television program, the "Today" show. The sponsor was a paint roller, which nobody had ever seen before. Dave Garroway had showmanship enough to have as his stooge a photogenic chimpanzee who could handle a paint roller. It saved the "Today" show and made him instantly famous as its anchor.

Such TV adventures seemed to pale, however, in comparison with Washington's offer of foreign travel, diplomatic intrigue, CIA subplots, military adventures, and vacations in the Alps. I suggested to my British wife that we might possibly be headed for a tour of duty in

Europe. After considering, for about three minutes, the prospect of moving from Falls Church, Virginia, to Paris with three children, a household of goods and possessions, and leaving behind a world of friends and community ties, she said simply, "Let's go." So we went.

14

Diplomacy in Paris

WE EAGERLY RETURNED to Europe after more than twelve years, and this time with a family in peacetime. Paris was to be our home for six years. We lived in a splendid townhouse in the sixteenth *arrondissement* within walking distance of the Bois de Boulogne. The mood in the city was tense when we arrived due to the plastic bomb epidemic brought on by the rage of Algerian-based French against metropolitan French who were intent on giving the Algerians their independence. But my official duties had nothing to do with Algeria.

In 1958 I was assigned by the U.S. Information Agency as public affairs assistant to the U.S. ambassador to NATO, the fifteen-nation conglomerate pieced together by the World War II Allies to keep Communist Russia out of Western Europe. Our ambassador was W. Randolph Burgess, a prominent banker. His wife, Helen, was the daughter of the former chief of police of Boston, from whom she had learned all the principles of an aggressive defense against any threat to public tranquility and order. To add to her formidable upbringing, Helen Burgess was a top officer in the Women's Army Corps. A portrait of her in full Army regalia hung over the fireplace in the ambassadorial residence. She once announced that she had proudly worn that uniform for four years, to which my ten-year-old daughter Phyllis was heard to reply, "It must have gotten awfully dirty." Fortunately for my prospects in the diplomatic corps, Mrs. Burgess was slightly hard of hearing.

Life in the *corps diplomatique* has its privileges. One skips across borders with the greatest of ease. Police of every country take a benign interest in one's convenience and well-being. While the world continued on its mad rush toward World War III with the Cuban missile crisis, the diplomatic service maintained its customary bland civility toward friend and potential foe alike—overtly, at least. My role was to inform the public media about NATO and help create a positive attitude toward NATO and, of course, toward the United States in particular. This led into projects both overt and covert. Oddly enough, in the war of public opinion, we had as much opposition from our ally France as we did from our adversary Russia. De Gaulle thought that NATO was unnecessary. He refused to attend NATO ceremonies and downplayed America's role in World War II. One was constantly reminded of Churchill's wartime comment to his aide: "Go find out what Charles is doing and tell him not to."

As the ambassador's assistant, my job was greatly facilitated by my being a full Army colonel and having a high-level diplomatic rank. And as one who participated in the liberation of Paris in 1944, I had a great and abiding interest in cultivating a friendly attitude among the French toward American foreign policy. My chief accomplices in this effort were the editors of several French journals and Pierre Emanuelli, a prominent member of the French delegation to NATO. Pierre became a close cohort in keeping the French Foreign Minister friendly toward us in spite of the antagonism of de Gaulle himself. Together, we sought out and befriended all the French editors we could find, hoping that the results would be a journalistic climate favorable to American interests. My intimacy with French journalism paid off when I was the first official among the delegations of NATO to receive reports of Kennedy's assassination, which came to me via Elie Maisse, a French journalist. His telephone call during our evening meal included the first of many condolences, official and unofficial, which came to us from our French friends. Taxi drivers, shopkeepers, policemen, bartenders, and unfamiliar folks in the street all offered expressions of sincere sympathy.

Ambassador Burgess presided over an entirely separate and quite different diplomatic post from that of the U.S. ambassador to France, Amory Houghton. While the U.S. Embassy in Paris had roots going back to the time of John Adams, Thomas Jefferson, and Ben Franklin, our embassy to NATO was largely an improvisation, dealing with the problems and personalities of fifteen different nationalities. This provided my family and me with a broad multinational social life that embraced both military and diplomatic protocol. Our household itself became an international community, which included a French seamstress, au pair students from England, Columbia, and America, piano teachers for my daughters from Germany and South America, and a coal man from Corsica. Additionally, we had our American connections. I was a member of the American Chamber of Commerce. My wife and I were active at the American Church of Paris where she directed the children's choir and I ushered, among other things. And, like most Americans living in Paris, we did not fail to frequent the Folies Bergeres or the Crazy Horse Saloon.

Members of the American business, diplomatic, and entertainment community living in Paris at that time banded together to form an American presence in the intellectual life of Paris. This grew into the concept of a college, which since that time has taken form as the American College in Paris. It was modeled on the American University of Beirut, Lebanon, which for years was the only American college abroad. As such, it offered a liberal arts curriculum with an emphasis in history. Today, the American College in Paris retains its status with American college accrediting organizations. I had the honor to be one of its founding trustees.

Every American congressman or senator who came to town ended up at our home, where we brewed up cocktail parties with Gaullist politicians, British field marshals, and international journalists from all the NATO countries. Art Buchwald, humorist for the *Herald Tribune*, was a frequent guest who helped us keep a properly balanced view of what was an almost unreal scene. Picture our drawing room with the hum of many languages, military men of every rank, and their wives trading stories with tipsy diplomats, journalists pumping diplomats and vice versa, and more pin-striped-suited spies than you can imagine. Edward R. Murrow, then director of the U.S. Information Agency, found ample opportunity at our home to both gather and dispense information. Jim Gavin, who had replaced Amory Houghton as U.S. ambassador to France, provided some military color to those occasions from his experiences as a parachutist general in the Battle of the Bulge.

Our entire family became bilingual, and my wife could argue with the local butcher in his own dialect. My two older daughters, Phyllis and Marilyn, went to the American School of Paris, a private school supported by the U.S. Embassy for the American community in Paris, while my third daughter, Allyson, now deceased, went to a local French kindergarten, where she became totally bilingual. Our vacations were taken either at the Army Center in Berchtesgaden for skiing, or touring through Germany, Scandinavia, and the United Kingdom where my wife's family provided us with a second home. Adding this safe haven to my former associations with England during World War II makes the United Kingdom my permanent, spiritual, sentimental second home.

During the Kennedy presidency, the usual diplomatic game of musical chairs took place, with my Republican Ambassador Burgess being replaced by a true New York Democrat, Thomas Finletter whose wife, Gretchen, was the daughter of Walter Damrosch, the famous conductor. For a brief period, while both families were in Paris, each day was marked by skirmishes between the two ambassadorial wives, who actually could not stand each other. I took advantage of a business mission to Iceland (a NATO member) during this period in order to avoid the warfare at the Embassy. On my return, the Finletters were firmly ensconced and since my position was nonpolitical, I resumed my normal duties. NATO weathered the storm.

After six years of government service in Paris, I began to wonder if this was, after all, "real life." The advantages to my three daughters were manifest. My wife had the French under control, and she was much nearer her family's home than she had been in Virginia. The Russians did not frighten her; she had seen the Germans off, and the Russians could not be any worse. England had recovered from the war and we had established and educated a happy cross-bred family with the best that the worlds of academia, business, the military, and official Washington had to offer. My question was, "Where do we go from here?"

15

New Era of Communications

HAVING TASTED THE delights of secret intelligence and high-level political intrigue and diplomacy, a return to NBC in New York and traditional broadcasting seemed a bit tame. My inclination after Paris was to return to Washington as soon as an opportunity presented itself. One did, and it put me into even more complex action involving the overt and covert business of government, the Cold War and all its ramifications, and interaction between the public sector, Congress, and the private sector of broadcasting industry.

It was 1964. Cracks were appearing in the Iron Curtain, and World War III now seemed less imminent. The influence of the Voice of America was being diluted by pervasive commercial broadcasting that carried one simple message, "spend your money and buy things," that everyone understood. Perhaps it was time for me to return to what was called "private business" and harness my patriotic inclinations to the good old vulgar profit motive. This is a well-known and widely practiced behavior pattern in Washington and all other political or industrial capitals. In career terms, it is known as "lobbying." One who has had experience in and with the upper levels of government bureaucracy can be very useful to those in the private sector where fortunes, personal and corporate, wax or wane depending on the mind-set of the bureaucrats. It was Madison Avenue all over again, wrapped in the flag and laced with bourbon.

In the middle of my decision-making process on what to do next, the government made a surprising move. It discovered Arthur C. Clarke, the British radio-astrophysicist and social philosopher.

Through some simple arithmetic, he had figured out that with state-of-the-art rocket technology, a communications satellite could be placed in a stationary orbit at precisely twenty-three thousand miles altitude. From there it could see one-third of the earth's surface and interconnect peoples and nations through wireless frequencies. Three of these satellite devices could cover the entire world.

To Clarke, to governments, and to the communications industry, the implications of such satellites were immediately obvious and threatening. Clarke wrote about these implications in his numerous science fiction novels. Others felt that no single sector or entity should be allowed to dominate this scenario. Conscious of the opportunities as well as the dangers, all interested parties joined hands as in a global square dance and circled first left and then right. They came up with a new concept for a joint public-private enterprise and established Intelsat, the global satellite consortium. The U.S. member of Intelsat, Communications Satellite Corporation (COMSAT), was itself a consortium of the U.S. government, Army, Navy, private businessmen, lawyers, politicians, scientists, investors, and me. Having survived life among all these crosscurrents, I was offered the position of executive assistant to the chairman of the board of COMSAT. My first mission there was to find out what the president of the company was doing and let the chairman know. The chairman was the former CEO of Standard Oil of New Jersey, Leo Welch; the president was former Secretary of the U.S. Air Force, Joseph Charyk. My reporting responsibilities became complex, but then I was used to such situations. In addition to these two, there was the Executive Office of the White House, which wanted to know what everyone was doing, and the FCC, which was supposed to supervise and regulate communications in this country but had not the foggiest idea as to how to operate either in outer space or over the surface of the earth where boundaries of states, nations, oceans, and continents had suddenly become obsolete. Arthur C. Clarke, who set all this in motion, took great delight in the resulting confusion. He had earned $36 for his historic essay, "Extra-Terrestrial Relays," which appeared in the British *Wireless World* in 1945. In it he presented his theory of stationary or synchronous satellites as well as displayed his disdain for anything below the level of pure science. A trillion-dollar industry was built on his idea and at the time enriched everybody concerned, including now Sir Arthur.

Most of the players in this opening game of the satellite era have long since departed. Looking back, I see them as talented, bewildered, but ambitious individuals, drawn together by a common desire to create something new, to escape earthly bonds for outer space, and to manipulate old institutions into a new world culture compatible with a new technology. This is the way it looked to me, and although my precise role in the whole scenario was uncertain, I felt that was exactly where I wanted to be.

Our director of operations at COMSAT was George Sampson, a retired Army general. The chief legal counsel was David Acheson, son of the former Secretary of State. The technical vice president, Sig Reiger, was a transplanted German rocket scientist. For public relations there was a journalist who contributed not a little toward whetting the public's appetite for buying COMSAT stock. And, in the background, there was still Arthur C. Clarke, whose writings meant as much to me as did much of the New Testament. If God had any explaining to do, Arthur was the one to do it for Him. Besides, Arthur has a great sense of humor, which helped me understand cosmic forces, infinity, gravity, relativity, and light speed. As for politics and economics, Arthur felt that these subjects were beneath the contemplation of educated men.

At COMSAT then, there were the front men with job titles and the ultimate responsibilities, and a sort of shadow cabinet whose duties were to keep their bosses out of trouble and to make sure that some kind of progress was being made. It was with the latter group that I found my mission for the next nine years.

Returning from Paris in 1964, our family made its home once again in Falls Church in a community called Lake Barcroft. Our three daughters were at home, in various stages of schooling. My wife, never one to confine herself to housekeeping, taught ballet in the local school system. I maintained an active role in the U.S. Army Reserves, prompted by a vague premonition that all wars were not over. I spent two weeks each summer at an Army camp, training mind and body in the martial arts and delivering lectures on the new era of satellite communications and its possible meaning to the armed services, especially the Special Forces at Ft. Bragg, North Carolina, to which I had a mobilization assignment.

The satellite era had begun. Other countries started to gear up and the International Satellite Consortium attempted to give order to the general chaos of the communications world in the late sixties. COMSAT, as the designated U.S. member, was the engine that ran the worldwide system. But it soon became apparent that at least as far as the U.S. was concerned, a domestic satellite carrier would be the best way to bring the advantages of satellite into the service of our public needs. The question was which of the domestic telecommunications carriers should take on the task, or should it fall to the quasi-public COMSAT enterprise. (COMSAT was partially subsidized by the government and also issued stock in the company.)

There followed a vast and furious battle for the U.S. domestic satellite franchise, a battle that COMSAT lost to RCA and Western Union. As a lobbyist in Washington, I failed to convince the White House that the domestic franchise should go to COMSAT, which, after all, was a creation of Congress. In this case, private industry won against aggressive bureaucrats. My efforts revealed to me, however, that the cable TV industry would become the major user of this new domestic satellite technology and would soon take its place among the broadcast network giants NBC, CBS, and ABC as an equal and creative rival. Up until now, the cable television industry was comprised of individual local operations. All of a sudden, with the use of Scientific Atlanta Earth Station receivers and satellites, it could become an interconnected network on a national scale. Connected only by land lines and transmitters, NBC, CBS, and ABC began to look like anachronisms.

The largest cable TV entity in the U.S. was Teleprompter Corporation in New York, which owned cable TV systems throughout the nation, each one a local operation with a headquarters or head-end connected by a land line to a national network. Teleprompter's chief technical vice president, the nationally known scientist and inventor of the Teleprompter device, H. J. Schlafly, was a frequent visitor to the University Club bar in Washington where most of our business was done. We struck up an acquaintance that determined the course of my remaining career. Schlafly understood the potential synergy between the cable television and the satellite industries. The Teleprompter chairman, Jack Kent Cooke, did not, however. So Schlafly suggested that together he and I should revolutionize the U.S. communications infrastructure by spreading the word about the miracles made possible by the ownership of a ten-meter-diameter satellite receiving station, a small investment in both hardware and property. All that had to happen was for the "dish" receiver to be able to "see" the satellite twenty-three thousand miles away in equatorial orbit without any obstruction. It usually took a cable TV owner less than five minutes to sign up for the dish once he grasped the idea that John Wayne was speaking to him direct from Hollywood via a single satellite in space, practically overhead. So, in the early seventies, I moved to Connecticut and joined Teleprompter, where Schlafly and I took a traveling satellite road show over much of the U.S. countryside. We demonstrated this new communications system using a dish mounted on a truck to receive a beam from the satellite in orbit.

In the course of this pilgrimage, we discovered how useful the satellite would prove to be in solving social problems. One day, certain Canadian authorities called us at Teleprompter to inquire whether they might have the use of our satellite equipment. The reason for the inquiry was the occurrence of riots among the forestry workers at James Bay in northern Canada. It seemed they had nothing to do in their time off, and the Canadian authorities thought that live television might be useful in calming the unrest. We agreed to make an earth station available that could communicate via the satellite that covered Canada. The earth station, a Scientific Atlanta dish or antenna, was duly trucked from the U.S. through a hitherto trackless forest to the logging camp at James Bay. The minute the television service was turned on, the labor riots subsided, management and workers received all the entertainment they could absorb, and both labor and entertainment history was made.

This promotional project was expensive, and the Teleprompter Corporation was not in financial health sufficient to the task. As the satellite entrepreneur for the company, I was the first casualty of this situation, and for the first time in my life found myself out of a job, but overloaded with readily marketable assets. I also had two daughters in college and one in high school plus a substantial suburban establishment to maintain. It was time to take a personal inventory. Economics had less to do with the situation than did the basic questions of who was I and where was I headed. It was definitely a turning point in my career, with a variety of options at hand but no clear perception of which path to take.

Everything up to the end of World War II seemed to have been preordained. Events took place in an orderly fashion. I did the best I could in the military, and it must have been acceptable because I rose in rank from private to lieutenant colonel at the war's end. When off duty I played every piano I could find, from one in a Belgium brothel to one in the field services of the Church of England on Sundays in Luxembourg. On only one occasion did music almost end my military career. In a village in eastern France, lately occupied by our foe, I found a player piano which, after being turned on, blew up. I was at a safe distance but hardly expected the Germans, with their love of music, to sink so low as to booby-trap a piano. Perhaps this was a warning, to steer me away from choosing a postwar musical career.

However, I still believe that if I had chosen to make a career in music, I would now be in Hollywood making music for movies, TV, and the live stage. Or I might now be a lawyer in the entertainment business, suing people for sins like copyright infringement. It had never occurred to me to take up acting even after that day at lunch in the London Officers Club during the war when Jack Warner asked me to take a screen test. I thought this was flattering but hardly the right thing to do at a time when my first duty was to help defeat the Germans, who were making frequent visits at night over London to defeat us. First things first.

Another career option would have been to stay in the Army. I had achieved enough rank to make this a comfortable prospect. Even in peacetime the Army had a clear mission, which was to get ready for the next war, which did not seem too far away. My Army assignment had been in signal intelligence, the most secret arm of all the intelligence services. Our war experience in this field had led to the creation of the largest secret service of all, now known as the National Security Agency (NSA) about whose work nobody was allowed to say anything. But secrets no longer held any attraction for me. I wanted to talk about my work, at least to my wife. I did, however, maintain a relationship with the Army through the reserves, in which I attained the rank of colonel. Using my vacation time in summer, I did duty in such exotic places as Oberammergau, at the U.S. Special Warfare School, Panmunjom in Korea, at conferences between North and South Koreans, and at the Pentagon, in the Psychological Warfare branch of the Joint Chiefs of Staff. I still wanted to be in uniform, at the right place and right time, for the next big shooting match.

The outcome of all my deliberations was that I put wars, politics, and secret operations to the back of my mind. Hub Schlafly suggested that we pool our knowledge and talents and try to remake the world into what we thought it ought to be. We would do this with our own corporate identity, which we christened "American Transcommunications Corp." with a mission to offer consulting services in the satellite and cable TV environment to a largely uninformed industry. Our efforts were welcomed, and we were beholden to no one. We took up the crusade to move America into the broadband-satellite era, an effort that continues today.

There were also avenues of opportunity for us in our allied calling, the cable TV industry. We had noticed that the entire "gold coast" of Connecticut had no cable TV service at all. A nearby friend, Charles Dolan of Long Island, had noticed the same thing. It was a simple matter to arrange a discussion between Dolan, already a multiple cable system owner, Jack Howard of the Scripps Howard dynasty, and ourselves. The outcome was the creation of Cablevision of Connecticut. We bid for, and won, the area cable franchise for ten towns in the state. Today, it is one of the most successful cable TV operations in the nation. Dolan's empire soon became the country's seventh-largest cable system, but this was the last entrepreneurial adventure for American Transcom. Other industry adventurers profited more, risked more, and now, in the current state of the telecommunications industry, have lost more. Some of them may even lose their freedom, as well as their friends, as angry stockholders sue and government regulators indict and prosecute.

Our company, American Transcom, became dormant well before this Pandora's Box was opened, due to the ages of its principals, who were now three in number, namely Schlafly, myself, and Howard Hawkins, a lawyer and former president of RCA Communications. We were pioneers in the interconnectedness of cable TV and communications satellites but could not stay to reap the harvest. It was just as well. The harvest had turned into a whirlwind. And with the multiplicity of program channels made available to satellite, the common denominator of taste sinks lower and lower, along with the stock market's evaluation of the industry. We three sometimes wring our corporate hands and wonder, What have we wrought? Arthur Clarke, his mind still fixed on outer space, would say, "I told you so."

We are retired now, which is just as well, for the telecommunications industry has spawned as likely a flock of con men, rogues, thieves, and white-collar criminals as ever appeared at a turn of history where fortunes are to be made, reputations ruined, investors fleeced, and workers plundered. Such is the current scenario.

Before I did retire, however, I had an unexpected opportunity to once again participate in the early pristine stage of developing a telecommunications system. The U.S. government had taken an interest in the Kingdom of Nepal, and wondered if I was available to travel thither to lend the Nepalese a helping hand in their slow crawl toward modernity by showing them how to install and operate a commercial cable television system hooked up to a South Asia–positioned communications satellite. China, through Tibet, was making menacing gestures and perhaps it would be better if we moved in first. Television could be the harbinger of influence over many facets of the local culture, and cable TV in particular could make our influence pervasive, or so we thought.

Thus, in 1994, the International Executive Service Corporation, a quasi-governmental entity, offered to send me to Kathmandu to get this project started. My wife, who had agreed to several migrations in the past, agreed once more, and we took off for the top of the world. While in Kathmandu I phoned Sir Arthur C. Clarke and was privileged to tell him that in bringing satellite-linked cable television to Nepal I was helping fulfill his 1945 prediction that satellite technology would abridge all national boundaries and cultures. Once again, he said, "I told you so."

Nepal, in the center of South Asia, is ideally situated to be a distribution center for programming and news for all that part of the world, and the officials there knew this. They were caught up in the belief that television would bring them fame and fortune—they hoped to become the Hollywood of the Himalayas. This beautiful country is predominantly Hindu and Buddhist with some Muslims all coexisting—trading gods, goddesses, snakes, and turtles to their mutual benefit. But there seems to be a fourth religion now, and (if it can be called that) it is "Development." The present generation of young businessmen pursue development with more fervor than they ever spent on Buddha, Shiva, or Vishnu. When I was there, my impression was that, while these gods may draw the tourists, development projects of all kinds are where the action is and traditional religion is becoming irrelevant. All faiths mingle in joint ventures and frequent the stock exchange, which for the few local Muslims has escaped the Prophet's prohibition on gambling.

While I participated in the third religion, my wife unexpectedly became "America's Singing Ambassador," as reported in an article of that title in *Greenwich Time*.

◆ ◆ ◆

Call her Mrs. Chips. Or Madame Teacher. Or the singing envoy.

But whatever you call her, Decima Knight Button is one heck of a representative for the United States. Decima, as many readers know, is the charming wife of Bob Button, the talented pianist, musical director of the Melody Men, and cable TV whiz. She is also a very gifted singer, having learned her trade performing in musicals on the London stage during WW II. That's where she met Bob, a young U.S. Army officer stationed in London. He came to her family's home one Sunday for dinner. When some of the guests asked Decima to sing, Bob volunteered to accompany her on the piano. And he's been doing it ever since.

Decima, for her part, has accompanied Bob on all sorts of adventures around the world, including his stint as director of the Voice of America right after WW II. A couple of months ago, she accompanied her peripatetic spouse on his latest adventure—two months in Nepal serving as a consultant for the International Executive Service Corps. When the IESC asked Decima to teach conversational English to the good burghers of Kathmandu, she said, "Fine!"

It turned out that many were already eagerly learning English at the American Language Institute, operated by the U.S. Information Agency, and their vocabulary and grammar was excellent. However, their casual conversation, or schmoozing skills, was limited, and how can one do business with an American without knowing how to schmooze? So, after each formal English class, she would meet with the students and just plain talk, without worrying about rules of grammar. After a while people began stopping Decima on the street, calling her "Madame Teacher," and asking to join her conversational sessions.

Students were not confused at all by the fact that Decima's proper British accent was vastly different from her husband's Americanese. They were there to learn popular expressions, vernacular, ordinary conversation and didn't care much whether it came wrapped in a London or middle American accent.

Decima Button. Survivor of the London blitz. And America's newest ambassador-at-large.

❖ ❖ ❖

And when my wife and I returned to Connecticut, it was as Nepal's newest unofficial goodwill ambassadors.

16

Connecticut Music

ON SEVERAL OCCASIONS I have asked myself whether I should have stayed in the Army. Well, the answer is obviously no. Much of the reason lies in the life my wife and I have created and live in Greenwich, Connecticut, built around community service and music. Of course, I am still in the Army Reserves and exchange salutes every time we visit an Army post, which, I admit, makes my day. But at my present age, the Army is not likely to summon me forth to battle Al Qaeda or the Iraqis. Still, I love that salute.

Music is my main preoccupation now, my inspiration, and personal pot of gold, as it always has been. It has insulated me from countless near-disasters. It found me a talented wife who is also my musical partner, just when I was about to propose to another lovely British girl who could not carry a tune. It has carried me around the world on cruise liners, into high circles of social life where music breaks up the hold of alcohol and boring conversation, and into religious services of every denomination. And most important of all, it has brought me the friendship of many people who love to sing and need an accompanist. Like my wife.

Greenwich has countless organizations devoted to music, some professional, some amateur. My modest share of this activity is on the borderline between the two. To begin with, there is my seventeen-piece Bob Button Orchestra—almost a continuation of what I was doing as a Dartmouth undergraduate in the thirties. We play the same tunes, which are now back in favor after sixty-five years. The same band arrangements that hypnotized crowds at Glen Island Casino and

Roseland Ballroom are all in fashion, and while leading the band in this activity, I do not feel any older now than I did then.

All the big bands had their singing groups in addition to their featured vocalists. Our soloist is Gail Clear, of Stamford, and exemplifies the style of the girls who sang with the Miller, Dorsey, Shaw, and Basie bands of that era. Our swing singers are six in number and carry the band's performances to new heights with their renditions of old favorites and their stage presence and charm. The concerts of this ensemble draw the townspeople in droves. When performing on their own, without the band, these six young ladies appear as "Button and Bows," a name I would not have chosen, but they like it. I play their accompaniment, write some arrangements for them, and try to arbitrate their disputes over what they are going to wear at concerts.

Also on my musical agenda are the Melody Men, a stalwart troop of sixteen members of the Retired Men's Association who are anything but retired when it comes to music. They march in to a concert, sing twelve numbers, shake hands with everybody, and march out again. This is one of the most popular events on the retirement home circuit. Their repertoire covers every musical standard from 1900 to today. Their mission is to make the audience forget about the passage of time. It is a kind of therapy. The message is simple—put away the pills and sing along with us. You will feel better right away.

The class act on the circuit is called Playmakers on Wheels, because it is an offshoot of Playmakers of Connecticut, the town's original dramatic society. These are prima donnas, divas, bassos profundos, and heroic tenors, soloists all, equally at home with an aria, a recitative, ballad, or blues. They are individual artists who only occasionally offer a duet or a trio. They are the salon act, the chamber music society of the town. My wife organizes their concert tours and programs. I do my best to keep up with their sometimes difficult accompaniments, last-minute changes of key, their dynamics and dispositions. As a one-man pit orchestra, I find this a very demanding but equally rewarding activity. The residents at the retirement homes are always responsive. We know we are filling one of the many empty spots in their lives, while we are completely out of empty spots in ours. Between rehearsals and performances, I have little time for anything else. Except, that is, for meetings of the local Lions Club, the Masonic Lodge, the Retired Men's Association, our church and its related activities, the Old Greenwich Yacht Club, and the care of our home. But these are all local activities.

On a broader scale, I should mention the High Arctic Explorers Club of Resolute Bay, Canada, of which I am a member. I had read about it and was determined to join it. In 1994 I journeyed to Resolute Bay via Montreal, a six-hour flight. (It took my ancestor, Admiral Sir Thomas Button, six months to get there and back.) Once there, one joins up with the next sled expedition to either the North Pole or the Magnetic Pole, each a trip of about four hundred miles over the ice, which is twenty feet thick. I chose the Magnetic Pole, to check out a legend. The Inuit, or Eskimos, believe that if you stand precisely at the Magnetic Pole for a few minutes, the electrical polarity of your body gets reversed, with unpredictable results. I thought this worth a try, and I am still analyzing the effects. They say it can turn Republicans into Democrats, introverts into extroverts, cure tone-deafness and color-blindness, and reverse one's losses at the gaming tables of Las Vegas. Aside from these mundane matters, the Inuit tour guide assured me that Magnetic Pole treatments are the best and surest aphrodisiac in the world.

A different spectrum of events presents itself as we consider our overseas connections. First among these is my wife's family, whose remaining members are scattered from Scotland to Sussex and Kent. My niece is a prominent Conservative member of the British Parliament from Beckenham. Periodically one or another of our relatives shows up at our home to renew family ties and our loyalties to the Queen. My wife, a U.S. citizen, is just as British now as she was the day we met. The Union Jack stands at our front entrance, and tea is served daily at 4 PM to the delight of friends and neighbors.

We frequently visit England and these occasions have begun to take on an interesting historical slant. It seems that H.R.H. the Duke of Kent has taken an interest in the preservation and development of Bletchley Park as a historical monument and educational asset to future generations. BP, or Station X, figured prominently in my wartime duties. As an interservice and diplomatic source of intelligence that shortened the war significantly, it deserves a place in both British and American annals. Its code-breaking activity continued through the Korean, Vietnamese, Gulf, and other wars, and the intelligence it provides has prevented or preempted several other wars, including the Cold War of recent memory. Meanwhile, the basic mission of BP continues through war and peace, although now at a different location.

The Bletchley Park Trust, aware that I was one of the few Americans ever to be initiated into its secrets, made contact and requested my participation with an American orientation in the activities of the trust. Here in Greenwich we have initiated an informal forum, the Enigma Club, founded on the community of interest among former intelligence operatives who had some relationship with Ultra or Magic intelligence during World War II. There are a few in our town. By the very secrecy of our work, there has never been a collegial forum where we could gather and swap lies about our glorious past. Now, in the interest of building a sense of how history is really made, we hope that the club will promote college curricula with visits to Station X and, best of all, further an understanding of where the media get the material with which they feed the public's understanding, or misunderstanding, of events that shaped the past and that continue to shape current history.

Another overseas point of contact is our family estate known as Dyffryn Gardens, in St. Nicholas, Wales. This was the home of Sir Thomas Button and his family for four hundred years, ending in the sixteenth century when Sir Thomas, then an admiral in the navy of Queen Elizabeth I, passed on. Sir Thomas's principal service to the Queen was to chase and capture whiskey smugglers in the Irish Sea, whose cargo then ended up in the Queen's coffers and kitchens. His estate, now owned by Glamorgan County, is used as a conference center, but anyone who presents himself at the gate as having been sent thither by a member of the Button family, British or American, receives a royal welcome and red-carpet hospitality. Naturally, this is always on our itinerary when we visit the UK Although the initials "RB" carved into the stone entrance of the chapel there stand for Deacon Robert Button of the fifteenth century deaconate, I prefer to think that they are there to welcome me when my time comes.

But my time has not yet come. It has passed me by at a rather close distance several times due perhaps to bad aim by the Germans, fortunate timing on my part, lucky coincidence, and maybe (I like to think) timely intervention by Someone I know only as my "Unseen Guide." But there is so much left to do. So much music to play or compose. So much community work to accomplish on behalf of neighbors and family and friends. So much help to give for the unfortunate people in a world burdened by greed, hunger, strife, and misery of all kinds. One has to keep on trying to make even a modest contribution to the situation, and I will not feel that my time has come until it is no longer possible for me to do this. It all adds up to the conclusion I reached in the middle of the Battle of the Bulge in 1944: it seems to me that God needs our help just as much as we need His.

✦   ✦   ✦

With music playing such a dominant chord in my life, permit me a recap and riff from that perspective. I was born into a musical environment where my mother was a classical concert pianist and hoped that I would be one too. She played for string quartets, church choirs, garden club teas, and for every soloist in town. I was placed under the tutelage of one Gertrude Hale, the town's oldest piano teacher and, not surprisingly, a devotee of Bach, Beethoven, and Brahms. I diligently but not enthusiastically cultivated their styles and played them at Miss Hale's recitals in Maplewood clubs and church halls. To me it was a mechanical but not aesthetic process. I did not realize that music, in any form, would shape my entire intellectual and philosophical outlook on life and form the backdrop for the various career paths that opened up to me.

I progressed from basic scales and arpeggios as one learns to read and write, without forming any views about the composers or authors. The first time I noticed the "thought content" of music was when I mastered the Methodist hymnal and realized that the hymns were offering me a guide to orderliness in my young life. I had paid no heed to spiritual education until I realized that it could be expressed in song—and song with some rather good melodies and lyrics at that. From "Jesus Loves Me This I Know" to Handel's "Messiah" then became a short trip rather than a long journey. Miracles related in the Bible became believable in music. Spiritual life became just as real as the material one and flavored my actions and ambitions.

I gained enough confidence and persistence from studying Beethoven to become president of my high school senior class. I learned enough depth and richness of expression from Brahms to earn high marks in writing prose for English classes as well as honors and distinction in these at college. Then came Wagner, and I plunged into sensual fantasies and dreams of other worldly powers.

The journey from Wagner to Irving Berlin was my musical salvation. I grasped the connection between music and everyday life. My ambition to become the Wotan of Wall Street was cooled by the Great Depression, and I learned in those years that making music was a more substantial contribution to humanity than making money. However, I very soon learned that one could do both at the same time, especially during a depression. People needed music. It was a kind of therapy. But it still seemed to hold no promise for me as a career, and I had to face a career choice that included music but did not depend on it. I had no ambition to be a musician—a composer or a performer. That was all in the background. There had to be something more substantial.

Music was just the off-stage accompaniment to business, to politics, or even to a military career.

The signposts of life are sometimes obvious, sometimes subtle. Thus, my career as a bank executive was cut short when my employers discovered I spent my evenings playing jazz piano in the local bars. I was fired. But the very next day I found that NBC needed people who liked the environment of both business and piano bars. I was hired.

The colonel of my draftee regiment in boot camp happened to love music. Suddenly my duties there switched from learning how to kill people to putting on shows to entertain them. This made both the colonel and the troops happy, and whenever the outfit had to move somewhere, the baggage train always included a piano carefully concealed beneath gunpowder and cannons.

Music was still the accompaniment to my life. At every turning point of my career path there seemed to appear a new leitmotif, a theme, as in a Wagner opera. Sometimes it would be in minor key, with an overtone of foreboding. At others it would have the clash of cymbals and a march tempo. It would promise either a *Gotterdammerung* or a Resurrection. I have yet to find out which will bring down the final curtain. Meanwhile the music that has always accompanied my life seems to be accelerating in tempo and reaching toward a crescendo in volume.

I sense the growing divisions in society between those who amass wealth far beyond their needs, on one hand, and the rest of the world, on the other; and the rotten odor of corporate chicanery offends my nostrils as I wander among the towers of Wall Street. Yet I have at times aspired to such wealth, status, possessions, and power and have tasted some of each. Somehow I have found it wanting. Only music seems to satisfy and explain everything else.

So what remains? There are the human relationships that I think go on beyond this life. There are thoughts to share without limit; there are those who need help and those who can give it. And around it all there is music, the music of life that I have always needed and tried to live by. Can you hear it?

Epilogue

ALL MY LIFE I have been occupied with the practice of communications, whether verbally or through music, intercepting the communications of bellicose Germans, exchanging ideas and impressions with the opposite sex by nonverbal means (such as telepathy), or adapting new technology to communications. And now we are in a world of universal instantaneous communications technology that will release either the best or the worst instincts in human personal relationships. At worst it will reduce our world to a level where the only communication will be by means of weapons of mass destruction, in which case there will be nobody left to communicate anything from or to. At best it will unite the globe in harmony.

Currently the communications ball is in play. On Wall Street, furtive financiers and covetous communication-industry moguls with their lawyers conspire to concentrate the entire industry into fewer and fewer hands. The object of all this is to make it possible for the smallest number of persons or corporations to control the largest aggregate of information we receive at the hands of the various segments of the industry, and to manipulate the fees we pay for their services.

In Washington, on the other hand, maneuvering is devoted to precisely the opposite goal. There, the acronym "D.C." might well stand for "decentralized communications," so that the basic right of every citizen to speak his or her mind, and all at the same time, is preserved, even if not heard above the resulting noise level. The remote-control silencer may become the most valued possession of our century unless Congress, in the interest of its own self-preservation, makes it illegal to use one.

Communications—whether as an art form, a message medium, or a sort of miracle technology—offers special enticements to the interceptors, the buggers, the prying eyes, the technical pickpockets, and especially to the so-called security services. In military, political, and industrial espionage today, ordinary run-of-the-mill spies and barroom agents have become obsolete due to the more reliable and productive electronic snooper. The task is made easier, too, since whatever is floating out there on the airwaves is fair game for all.

Intercepting communications, in which I had an unexpected wartime part, came into full flower during the late unpleasantness with Germany and Japan in World War II. While it is said that successful Allied code-breaking shortened the war by at least two years, at the same time it broadened the outreach of the intercept intelligence business to international and global dimensions. The ultimate result may be that distinctions between friendly and hostile nations, all of whose communications systems have become transparent, will no longer exist. Everyone will be so preoccupied with listening in on and deciphering the plots and counter plots of their neighboring family, state, tribe, clan, or nation that no one will want to break up the fun by initiating any military action. After all, that would reveal the source of the information, and this is the unacceptable, cardinal sin in the intercept community. If this prognostication is at all accurate, we may witness the full potential of the communication industry's destiny to help bring about peace among peoples who really prefer curiosity to combat. Unless, that is, some hostile aliens from outer space are even now listening to our communications satellites, not for the next episode of "Star Trek", but to plan their next intergalactic conquest.

But that is another story. In this memoir I prefer reminiscence to prophecy. I have tried to recall where I have been rather than project where I am going. I hope you have enjoyed the journey.

0-595-32157-7

Printed in the United States
95385LV00004B/175/A